THE MICRO MEN

THE UNPRODUCED SCREENPLAY

IB MELCHIOR

The Micro Men: *The Unproduced Screenplay*
© 2013 Ib Melchior. All Rights Reserved.

No part of this book may be reproduced in any form or by any means, electronic, mechanical, digital, photocopying or recording, except for the inclusion in a review, without permission in writing from the publisher.

 Published in the USA by:
BearManor Media
PO Box 1129
Duncan, Oklahoma 73534-1129
www.bearmanormedia.com

ISBN 978-1-59393-389-0

Printed in the United States of America.
Book design by Brian Pearce | Red Jacket Press.

INTRODUCTION

In early 1958, I was contacted by a prominent surgeon in Philadelphia, whose name was Victor P. Satinsky. Dr. Satinsky's avocation was creative entertainment, and he had already dabbled in writing poetry and plays for the stage and was now becoming interested in motion pictures and had decided to produce a film of his own. He wanted a sci-fi film, not a BEM film — *Bug Eyed Monster* film — but something different, unusual, possibly with a medical theme, but he did not feel confident enough in his own know-how to write it himself and was looking for someone to do the job for him. Somehow he had learned that I was a science fiction writer and had taken a premedical course at the University of Copenhagen, and he felt I might be his man…

As fact would have it, in my own research, I had just learned a fact that impressed the stuffing out of me. I found out that every one of us is the host to a mass of independently living organisms — such as microbes and bacteria — a mind-boggling hundred trillion of them in our digestive tract alone, not to mention a like number on our skin and else where, living a mutually beneficial, symbiotic existence with us; they are living off us and in turn aid and regulate our physical functions and provide some protection against harmful invaders. In essence, as beneficial a relationship as could have been thought out. And here it was — my key to a really unusual sci-fi story. What if these microorganisms, living symbiotically with us, *were* sentient? Could actually "think" things out? And *The Micro Men* was born…

My Micro Men, however, were not of the homegrown kind. They came from somewhere out there, where they had evolved spectacularly, their space vessel crashing on earth 50,000 years ago, being swallowed by and imprisoned in a tar pit. The occupants went into a dormant spore existence, set free when brought up today by an oil drilling team, to —

But of course, you will read about that in the script. Victor loved the script and at once set out to tackle the really difficult part in film making, getting adequate financing and distribution. I suppose the task became too much for him. Months went by with no action, and finally the project was abandoned and the rights to the script reverted to me. I remember also putting out some feelers — but I was busy with other projects. The film was never produced.

Ib Melchior

"THE MICRO MEN"

Screenplay
by
Ib Melchior

The Coppage Company
3369 Canton Lane
Studio City, CA 91604
(818) 980-8806

1958
Reg. WGAW

"THE MICRO MEN"

FADE IN:

1   EXT. - DAY - WIDE ESTABLISHING SHOT - (MINIATURE)

We are in a valley; in the background weird and wild looking rock formations rise from the valley floor; the vegetation is sparse and hardy appearing; in the foreground a large, black tar pit bubbles slowly; in the far distance the smoke from a volcano can be seen; a couple of mastodons are grazing peacefully near the tar pit; further in the background is a small herd of bison; a dead camel or giant ground sloth lies near the edge of the tar pit half submerged in the viscous mass; nearby a group of teratornis vultures is tearing at the carcass of a wild horse...

Over the scene we superimpose the legend:

> Sharktooth Mountain, California
>
> 50,000 Years Ago

2   MED. SHOT - MASTODONS - (STOCK)

They are eating contentedly.

3   MED. WIDE SHOT - BISON HERD - (STOCK)

They, too, are grazing peacefully.

4   MED. CLOSE SHOT - VULTURES - (STOCK)

They are tearing away at the dead horse, squabbling shrilly among themselves.

5   CLOSE SHOT - DEAD ANIMAL IN TAR PIT - (MINIATURE)

The viscous tar is slowly bubbling around it.

6   WIDE SHOT - AREA - (MINIATURE) - (SPECIAL EFFECT)

Suddenly a high pitched whine intrudes upon the peaceful scene; a brilliantly glowing object streaks across the sky to land with a tremendous crash in the tar pit.

(CONTINUED)

6   (CONTINUED)

    sending the black, viscous tar spurting upwards in a
    great, glistening column, to fall back into the pit,
    heaving and seething...

7   MED. SHOT - MASTODONS - (STOCK)

    They trumpet in fright.

8   MED. WIDE SHOT - BISON HERD - (STOCK)

    With thundering hoofs they stampede.

9   MED. SHOT - VULTURES - (STOCK)

    Screeching and shrieking they frantically take wing,
    leaving the half eaten carcass.

10 MED. SHOT - MASTODONS - (STOCK)

    Trumpeting their alarm they run away in stif-legged
    fear.

11 MED. SHOT - TAR PIT - (MINIATURE)

    In the f.g. lies the dead animal, half submerged; the
    pit is boiling with lazy agitation; CAMERA ZOOMS IN to
    a CLOSE SHOT of the bubbling oozing tar surface under
    which the object from the sky has disappeared; it is
    belching huge, slow gas bubbles...

    Over this scene we super our Main Title:

                    THE MICRO MEN

    ...followed by the rest of the titles and credits.
    With the last credit we -

                                        DISSOLVE:

12 EXT. VALLEY - DAY - WIDE ESTABLISHING SHOT

    The topography of the place is very much the same as
    the opening shot. (NOTE: The miniature should be
    built to conform to the environment of this location.)

                                        (CONTINUED)

3.

12   (CONTINUED)

The CAMERA PANS the scene; the vegetation is of a familiar kind, still sparse; the mountains in the background have lost a little of their weirdness, and the distant volcano is long since extinct. As the CAMERA reaches the space once occupied by the tar pit, we see that this landmark long since has disappeared; instead we see an oil drilling rig at the exact spot...This is <u>Sharktooth Mountain</u> -- today; and a new oil well is being sunk...

It is a Rotary Rig; we identify the derrick, the engine housing, the boilers, the slush pit...It is obviously a fairly recently spudded in well; a couple of trucks and two or three cars are parked nearby. There is an air of tension and emergency activity in the air; the roughnecks and roustabouts are clustered excitedly around the Rotary Table on the Derrick Platform; the Kelly is in the hole, but is not rotating...

13   CLOSER ANGLE

We see a sign on the rig reading: SHARKTOOTH DAWSON #1. In the f.g. the roughnecks are gathered around the rotary table; they are muttering worriedly among themselves; Tim Hawkes, the Driller in charge of Sharktooth Dawson #1, is standing tensely at the lever at the Driller's Stand. Tim is a big, rough man in his late forties, who wouldn't hurt a fly. A roughneck, Hank, steps back from the square kelly; he goes over to Tim.

                    HANK
          All set, Tim!

14   TWO SHOT - TIM AND HANK

                    TIM
                 (grimly)
          Okay...We'll try the diamond bit
          this time - at 450 revolutions...
          that ought to do it...

                    HANK
          Hope so...I've never before seen
          a chrome steel rock roller bit
          twisted to pieces - in a couple
          of seconds!..

                    TIM
          Stand by! Here she goes!..

15 WIDER ANGLE - DERRICK FLOOR

   Hank walks to the rotary table; Tim activates the machinery; all the men are watching expectantly; slowly Tim lowers the new bit - which is guided by Hank - into the hole until the kelly is engaged in the rotary table bushings; he puts his hand on the rotating lever. There is not a sound except the steady, rhythmic whirr of the drilling engine.

16 CLOSEUP - TIM

   He looks grim.

17 CLOSEUP - HANK

   He looks tense.

18 CLOSEUP - ROUGHNECK - (PIPE-RACKER)

   He looks worried, expectant.

19 CLOSEUP - ANOTHER ROUGHNECK - (CATHEAD MAN)

   He, too, looks on edge.

20 CLOSE SHOT - TIM

                TIM
             (quietly)
        Here goes...

   Resolutely he brings down the lever and starts the rotating.

21 CLOSE SHOT - DRAW WORKS AND ROTARY CHAIN

   They begin to move...

22 CLOSE SHOT - ROTARY TABLE AND KELLY

   They begin to rotate...

23 DERRICK FLOOR - MED. SHOT

   All the men are watching the rotating turntable and kelly; almost at once the hollow rumble from below

(CONTINUED)

23   (CONTINUED)

turns into the hideous, penetrating screech of metal being torn asunder; then - suddenly - there is a loud screeching whine and a sharp snap like a gun report from the drill hole.

> HANK
> (shouting frantically)
> Twist-off! Twist-off!!!

Tim immediately stops the rotating, as the startled men automatically draw back from the rotary table.

24   CLOSE SHOT - TIM

He looks stricken; his jaw sets in grim realization; he hits the lever to bring up the kelly and drill pipe.

> TIM
> Round trip! Let's go!...

25   MED. SHOT - ROTARY TABLE

The men are grouped around it; the kelly is rising from the hole - followed by the drill ipe; just above the drill collar the pipe has been twisted apart...the drill collar and bit are lost in the hole!

Tim strides hurriedly to the broken drill pipe; he examines it carefully; Hank looks on.

> HANK
> Twisted like a pretzel! What's down there!?...

26   TWO SHOT

> TIM
> (grimly)
> Beats me, Hank...But we've got to get through - whatever it is!
>
> HANK
> (frowning in awe)
> I've been drilling for seventeen years - and I've never run into anything hard enough to twist off a diamond bit...

(CONTINUED)

26   (CONTINUED)

                    TIM
          You have now! We'd better start
          fishing for that tool - lost down
          there...

27   CLOSEUP - TIM

     He is frowning.

                              DISSOLVE:

28   EXT. UNIVERSITY CAMPUS GATE - DAY - MED. LONG SHOT

     It is an iron grill gate set in two massive brick or
     stone gate posts; above the gate a sign can be seen;
     it reads:

                    HEATHERTON UNIVERSITY

     A high wall stretches away on both sides of the gate.
     Leaning against one of the heavy stone pillars a young
     man is sitting on a stone - apparently enjoying the
     lovely day; it is Arthur Corliss, Doctor of Physics
     at the University, specializing in metallurgy; he is a
     masculinely handsome man in his late twenties. A small
     sports car drives up to the gate and stops; it is
     driven by a lovely, fresh looking young girl about
     twenty-one, Tim's daughter, Diane Hawkes. Art gets up
     and walks over to the car during:

                    DIANE
              (waving cheerfully)
          Hi, Art!..Sorry I'm late...
              (she opens the car
               door)
          Hop in!

     Art goes to the car and gets in, during:

                    ART
          Hi, Dee...What took you so long?

                    DIANE
          It's such a beautiful day...

28   TWO SHOT

                    ART
          Can't you ever be on time?...

                              (CONTINUED)

28   (CONTINUED)

>   DIANE
>   (she laughs)
> Dr. Corliss! I'm a woman...I'm not like one of your scientific experiments! I don't run like a clockwork!

>   ART
> I waited for you out here for almost half an hour...

>   DIANE
>   (cheerfully)
> Do you good! You can't be couped up with Professor Watkins in that musty old research lab of yours <u>all</u> the time...

>   ART
> Where do you want to go?

>   DIANE
> Let's take a ride down to the well and see Dad...

>   ART
> Must we?

>   DIANE
> Now, Art...Dad looks forward so much to our visits...

>   ART
> I just hope I'll have you to myself <u>some</u> of the time - after we're married...

>   DIANE
>   (quietly)
> Aren't you getting a little ahead of yourself?

>   ART
> I don't think so.

>   DIANE
> Art. You know I haven't given you my answer yet.

>   ART
> And <u>you</u> know, I won't take <u>no</u> for an answer!

(CONTINUED)

28 (CONTINUED - 2)

   Diane looks at him seriously; then she smiles; she
   starts up the car.

                    DIANE
            Hold on to your hat!..

   She steps on the starter; the little car comes to life
   with a mighty roar...

                                      CUT TO:

29 EXT. DERRICK - DAY - CLOSE SHOT - DRAW WORKS

   The engine is running full blast; pistons are stamping
   up and down; drums and chains are clattering along; it
   is quite a racket.

30 MED. CLOSEUP - TIM

   He is playing skillfully on the clutch controlling the
   hoist; he looks alert and satisfied.

31 EXT. DERRICK AREA - DAY - LONG SHOT

   The men are working on the derrick floor; Diane's car
   comes driving onto the area and stops near the derric;
   Diane and Art get out and approach the derrick.

32 CLOSER ANGLE - DERRICK LADDER

   Art and Diane get to the ladder and start climbing up
   to the derrick floor.

33 WIDER ANGLE - ACROSS TIM IN F.G. TO TURNTABLE IN CENTER
   AND DERRICK STEPS IN B.G.

   Hank and a couple of other roughnecks are standing
   around the hole; a heavy wire is slowly rising out of
   the drill hole pipe; Hank is watchfully observing its
   progress; in the b.g. Diane and Art climb up the
   derrick steps to the floor and walk over to Tim during:

                    HANK
                  (calling)
            Easy!..Easy!..

                                      (CONTINUED)

33   (CONTINUED)

Tim slows the hoist to a near stop; he is watching the weight indicator dial closely.

          HANK
        (calling)
    Okay!..Go ahead!..

Tim starts the wire moving up again; Diane and Art come up to him.

34   THREE SHOT

          DIANE
    Hi Dad!..How's everything?

          TIM
        (working the
        levers)
    Hi, kids!..Had a little trouble...
    I ruined a couple of bits - and
    lost a tool in the hole...the
    diamond bit...twisted off...

          ART
        (he looks
        astonished)
    How deep are you?

          TIM
    'Bout a hundred feet...

He indicates a ten foot core tray lying on the derrick floor; a fresh core sample still rests in it.

          TIM (cont'd)
    We just took our first core...

CAMERA PANS Art as he kneels down to examine the earth core in the tray.

          TIM (O.S.)
    We're drilling through an old tar
    pit...Those bone fragments are
    about 50,000 years old...

Art stands up.

          ART
    How'd you lose the tool?

                      (CONTINUED)

34   (CONTINUED)

                    TIM
           Some kind of large boulder block-
           ing the straight...We're bringing
           it up now...Here it comes!

35   REVERSE ANGLE - ACROSS TIM, ART AND DIANE IN F.G. TO
      DRILL HOLE

      The wire emerges slowly from the hole lifting out a
      large, mud-covered boulder held firmly by three-
      pronged, sawtoothed tongs; the boulder is about four
      feet long and two feet wide.

36   CLOSER ANGLE

      The boulder emerges completely; Hank and another rough-
      neck grab hold of it and swing it out to the derrick
      floor; it is slowly and carefully lowered down until
      it rests on the wooden flooring; the men look at it in
      awe, muttering among themselves. Tim comes in to the
      picture followed by Diane and Art.

                    TIM
           Let's see what we've got here...
                (to Hank)
           Play the hose on it...

                    HANK
           Okay...

      He moves to get the hose.

37   CLOSEUP - TIM

      He frowns at the boulder.

                    TIM
                (letting the
                 thought trail)
           I - wonder...

38   TWO SHOT - ART AND DIANE

      They look at each other and smile.

11.

39   WIDER ANGLE

Hank arrives with the hose; everyone draws back a little from the boulder as Hank begins to play a stream of water on the mud-caked object.

40   CLOSE SHOT - OBJECT

The mud is beginning to wash off; the vague shape of a definite object is starting to show through.

41   CLOSE TWO SHOT - ROUGHNECKS

They watch with curiosity, in silence.

42   CLOSEUP - TIM

He looks apprehensive; he frowns.

43   TWO SHOT - ART AND DIANE

They watch curiously; slowly their smiles vanish.

44   CLOSE SHOT - OBJECT

Almost all the mud has been washed off...The object can be plainly seen: It is shaped like an elongated egg about four by two feet in size and with two smooth symetrically protruding bumps at one end...The last dirt is washed off and the 'thing' is fully revealed... It is <u>completely smooth, jet-black...and shiny!</u>

45   TIGHT GROUP SHOT

Everyone is watching the object with amazement and incredulity; Tim looks very worried; Art extremely interested...

46   WIDER, LOW ANGLE ACROSS OBJECT LOOMING IN F.G. TO GROUP

They are all staring at the black, shiny 'thing'...Tim finally breaks the awed silence.

                    TIM
         Look at <u>that</u>, will you!..What on
         earth is <u>it</u>?

(CONTINUED)

46   (CONTINUED)

                    HANK
          It's no rock - that's for sure!

                    TIM
          What do you make of it, Art?

                    ART
                 (slowly)
          It's not a natural object...

                    DIANE
          You mean - it's man made?

                    ART
                 (soberly)
          Let's put it this way - somebody
          made it...yes...

                    TIM
          Then what's it doing in the middle
          of a 50,000 year old tar pit for-
          mation?

                    ART
          I - don't know...

                    HANK
          There weren't any people on earth
          50,000 years ago, was there, Doc?

                    ART
          No...Not as we think of them...That
          was the time of the Neanderthal Men...
          But they were more like great apes...
          They certainly could never make any-
          thing like - that!..

                    TIM
                 (uncertain)
          I wish I knew what it was....

47   ANOTHER ANGLE

     Art walks over to the object; he kneels to examine it.

                    ART
          It's made of some kind of metal...
                 (he turns to Tim)
          You tried to drill through this
          thing with the diamond bit, you
          said?

                                        (CONTINUED)

47   (CONTINUED)

>   TIM
>   Sure did.

Art runs his hand over the smooth object.

>   ART
>   (incredulously)
>   And there isn't a mark on it!
>   Not a scratch!
>   (he stands up;
>   slowly)
>   It isn't possible!..A metal as hard
>   as that just doesn't exist - not
>   on earth!

>   TIM
>   (apprehensively)
>   Well, if it weren't made on earth
>   - where <u>did</u> it come from?...<u>And
>   who made it</u>?

Art shakes his head.

>   DIANE
>   What - what does it mean, Art?...

>   ART
>   I don't know...But one thing is
>   certain...it is a fabulous find!

>   TIM
>   (worried)
>   I don't like it...not a bit...

>   ART
>   Okay. We'll take it down to the
>   University...Professor Watkins and
>   I can shelve our project for a
>   while...It's the perfect spot...
>   We can really study it there...What
>   do you say?

>   TIM
>   (uneasy)
>   I don't know, Art...

>   ART
>   Come on - let's get this thing on
>   a truck!..

>   DISSOLVE:

14.

48   EXT. THROUGH GATE TO UNIVERSITY CAMPUS - DAY - LONG SHOT

   It is a small university; the campus grounds are beautifully landscaped and kept; the buildings look more like old mansions than modern halls of learning.

                                          DISSOLVE:

49   EXT. SCIENCE BUILDING - DAY - LONG SHOT

   The building stands off by itse;f it is surrounded by the high brick wall (or iron fence) with the gateway; the front entrance to the three or four story building has a few steps leading up to the door.

50   INSERT - PLAQUE SET IN WALL

   It reads:

                   INSTITUTE OF SCIENCE

51   LONG SHOT - SCIENCE BUILDING

   CAMERA PANS up and ZOOMS in towards a row of windows on the third floor.

                                          DISSOLVE:

52   INT. THIRD FLOOR CORRIDOR - DAY - MED. CLOSE SHOT - DOOR

   On it can be seen the legend:

                   PHYSICS LABORATORY B

53   INT. LABORATORY - DAY - CLOSE SHOT - ACETYLENE TORCH

   Its jet of white hot cutting flame splashes against the black surface of the object from space.

54   WIDE SHOT - B LABORATORY

   The large room is a typical laboratory devoted to the study of the science of physics; there are several large tables; an abundance of equipment and apparatus; a couple of sinks; cabinets, racks, drawers and shelves.

                                          (CONTINUED)

15.

54   (CONTINUED)

The curious object lies on a large table; surrounding it at a little distance stand Art, Tim, Diane and Professor Stewart Watkins. Watkins is the Dean of Science of the University; he is in his late fifties, an excitable, enthusiastic little man with a wide temperament range, the reach of which he often encompasses in a short span of time; yet he is a top scientist and a clear thinker...

A young man wearing a face shield and a leather chest apron is playing the acetylene torch on the object on the table - apparently to no avail; he shuts off the torch - the flame dies with a hiss; he lifts his face plate.

55   CLOSEUP - BRYAN

He wipes his face with the back of his hand; he is Bryan Kenmore, a handsome, alert young man in his early twenties; he is a graduate science student specializing in biochemistry, and doing post graduate work at the Heatherton University with Professor Watkins during the summer months.

56   CLOSE GROUP SHOT

Bryan cautiously reaches out his hand and touches the object at the spot where he has been applying the cutting flame from the torch.

            BRYAN
Won't do, Professor Watkins...It isn't even warm!

Watkins impatiently steps up to the object; he feels it.

           WATKINS
Fantastic...Utterly fantastic!..
A metal that doesn't conduct heat!..

He bends to peer at the spot.

           WATKINS
Not a mark on it!

He straightens up and turns to Bryan.

           WATKINS
You can put that torch away, Bryan...

(CONTINUED)

56 (CONTINUED)

Watkins alternately talks to the others and examines the object; Bryan puts the acetylene torch away and takes off his face shield; he begins to untie the strings on his back holding the protective apron in place, during:

          WATKINS
...It has resisted every cutting tool...every acid test...heat...abrasion...and we haven't even nicked it!

          ART
I'm certain it's some kind of metal alloy - although I've never seen anything like it...That's why I...

          WATKINS
        (interrupting)
Yes, yes...I agree with you...This object was not made on earth...

He turns and bends over the 'thing' to examine it closely with Art, while Tim, who has lost some of his awed apprehension, looks on with interest; Diane notices that Bryan has trouble untying the knot in the apron strings on his back; she walks over to him.

57 TWO SHOT

          DIANE
        (with a smile)
Here...Let me help you...

Bryan looks at her with obvious admiration.

          BRYAN
Thanks...

He turns his back so Diane can work on the stubborn knot.

          BRYAN
...I could use a couple of fingers - other than thumbs!..

          DIANE
        (with a little
        laugh)
I don't guarantee anything!

                          (CONTINUED)

57   (CONTINUED)

She starts to work on the knot.

           DIANE
I'm Diane Hawkes...

           BRYAN
Bryan Kenmore.

           DIANE
Are you also helping Professor Watkins with his research?

           BRYAN
        (grinning)
In a way!...I'm doing post graduate work with the Professor...

           DIANE
In metallurgy? Like Art?

           BRYAN
No. Biochemistry...I'm working on an antibiotics potentiator...

           DIANE
I'm afraid you lost me...I don't even know what it means!..

           BRYAN
        (smiling)
I'm looking for a chemical compound that when added to the antibiotics - like penicillin or the mycin group - will make them many times stronger - more effective...

           DIANE
Oh...Sounds very important...

           BRYAN
I think it is...

Diane has untied the knot.

           DIANE
There...

Bryan removes the apron.

           BRYAN
Thanks again.

They look at each other; Bryan has an obvious, instant liking for the girl.

58 WIDER ANGLE

Watkins turns from the object.

                WATKINS
        There's nothing further we can
        do until we get our equipment
        ready...
                (to Bryan)
        Bryan...Will you give Dr. Corliss
        a hand...

CAMERA DOLLIES in towards the jet-black, smooth object from space.

                WATKINS (cont'd)
        We'll start a series of electro-
        magnetic tests first thing to-
        morrow...

                DISSOLVE:

59 INT. B LABORATORY - DAY - CLOSE SHOT - OBJECT - PULL BACK TO MED. SHOT

Bryan, Watkins and Art are working with the space object; they are experimenting with magnetism and induced magnetic fields; there are several electromagnetic instruments, meters and apparatus around. The object, itself, is suspended between two sturdy clamps above a large, tubular wire coil, a solenoid to create magnetic fields; the electric current can be regulated on a small resistor, which is operated by Bryan.

It is a warm summer day, and a strong electric fan is turned on to give the men some relief from the heat; its steady drone can be heard throughout. Watkins is making some minor adjustment of the coil position; he straightens up; as he talks he indicates...

                WATKINS
        There...We'll try it in this posi-
        tion...The magnetic field of
        solenoidal current will travel -
        lengthwise...

He steps back; the three scientists regard the black object solemnly.

                WATKINS
        Start the current, Bryan...

60   CLOSER ANGLE

Bryan moves the control switch and a low humm makes itself heard, the three men watch the object tensely.

                    WATKINS
          More current!

Bryan moves the switch; the humm gets steadily higher in tone until it turns into a high-pitched whine; the men watch tautly; nothing visible happens.

                    WATKINS
          More!

                    BRYAN
          That's it...The limit!

Watkins looks annoyed.

                    WATKINS
          All right, all right...Cut it!

Bryan turns off the current; the whine dies away.

61   WIDER ANGLE

                    ART
          Perhaps the magnetic field itself
          is affected in some way by the
          object...

                    WATKINS
          Perhaps...We'll see...Bryan...The
          plate, please...I'll get some iron
          filings...

Art and Bryan place a thin white cardboard sheet between the solenoid coil and the object, fastening it in place, while Watkins gets a laboratory bottle filled with tiny iron filings; these he sprinkles evenly all over the cardboard during:

                    ART
          This had better work...

                    BRYAN
          I think maybe we ought to turn
          this thing over to one of the big
          Government Labs...

                                        (CONTINUED)

61   (CONTINUED)

                    ART
                (sharply)
            And be cheated out of the credit!?
            Not on your life!

                    BRYAN
            They're better equipped...

                    ART
            Look, Bryan. Suppose you leave
            the decisions to us...This is my
            - our big chance. I won't give
            it up.

62   ANOTHER ANGLE

                    WATKINS
            Dr. Corliss, will you take the
            transformer?

                    ART
            Of course...

He goes to the transformer.

                    WATKINS
                (nodding to Art)
            All right.

Art turns on the current - all the way up; the whine is heard above the drone of the electric fan. Watkins and Bryan watch the iron filings on the cardboard; Watkins begins to tap the sheet gently with his finger.

63   CLOSE SHOT - OBJECT AND CARDBOARD SHEET

As Watkins taps the sheet the iron filings quickly move to form streak patterns along the familiar geometrical lines of force of a magnetic field of solenoid current.

64   WIDER ANGLE

                    WATKINS
                (he grunts)
            ...The lines of force appear to
            be quite normal...

                                        (CONTINUED)

64   (CONTINUED)

                    BRYAN
          How about changing the direction
          of the field? How about running
          the helix at a right angle to the
          object?

                    WATKINS
          We'll try it...Dr. Corliss...

Art moves the coil under the object at right angles to
the object itself - placing it near the front end,
where the two bumps can be seen.

                    ART
          There...We'll try it at this end
          first...

Watkins begins to tap the cardboard; all three men are
watching the pattern made by the iron filings change.

65   CLOSE SHOT - OBJECT AND CARDBOARD SHEET

        As Watkins is tapping, the iron filings arrange them-
        selves in the same pattern as before - but now running
        at a right angle to the object...

        Suddenly a circular area of the size of a saucer on the
        side of the object begins to change color - getting
        lighter and lighter...All at once it begins silently
        and slowly to rotate.

                    WATKINS
          Look at the pattern...normal...

66   TIGHT GROUP SHOT

        The men are all looking closely at the cardboard and the
        filing pattern, they do not notice the moving area on
        the object.

                    WATKINS
                    (disappointed)
          Turn it off, Dr. Corliss...

        Art turns to carry out his instructions; suddenly Bryan
        looks up and sees the light-colored, slowly rotating
        circular area on the object; he grabs hold of Art.

                    BRYAN
          Wait! Look!!...

        The three men stare transfixed at the object.

67 CLOSE SHOT - OBJECT

The disc in its side continues to rotate; as it does it seems to screw itself outwards.

68 CLOSEUP - BRYAN

He watches tensely; he looks both excited and apprehensive.

69 CLOSEUP - ART

He frowns; he looks startled - almost stunned.

70 CLOSE SHOT - OBJECT

The rotating area is now over an inch from the surface of the object.

71 CLOSEUP - WATKINS

His face is aglow with interest and fascination.

72 TIGHT GROUP SHOT

The three men watch the object as if spellbound; all of a sudden the circular area - by now protruding almost two inches from the smooth surface of the object - swivels aside to hang from the rim of a perfectly round hole in the side of the 'thing'!

              WATKINS
Cut it! Cut the current!...

Automatically Art obeys...Bryan peers into the opening.

              BRYAN
           (excitedly)
It's hollow!..Some kind of container...

              WATKINS
           (to Art)
Dr. Corliss! The flashlight...In the drawer...

Art quickly takes out a flashlight from a drawer in front of him; he hands it to Bryan; Bryan shines the light into the opening.

(CONTINUED)

72   (CONTINUED)

                    BRYAN
          It's a small compartment...It's
          studded with little knobs...It's
          empty...No...there seems to be
          some kind of dust on the bottom...

He straightens up.

                    WATKINS
                 (to Art)
          You'd better shut off the fan...

Watkins hands a small brush to Bryan and himself holds a
shallow glass test bowl to the rim of the hole in the
space object. Art goes to shut off the big electric
fan - then returns to the two others during:

                    WATKINS
          Here...Use this...

73   CLOSE TWO SHOT

Bryan carefully begins to sweep out the dust into the
bowl held by Watkins.

                    WATKINS
          Careful, now...

                    BRYAN
          Looks like fine, black sand...

74   WIDER ANGLE

Art joins Watkins and Bryan again; all the dust has been
swept out; there is about a handful of it in the bowl;
Watkins holds it up close; peers at it curiously.

                    WATKINS
                 (triumphantly)
          Matter from space, gentlemen!
          Matter from space which arrived
          on earth over 50,000 years ago!

He holds the glass bowl up to the light - to peer at it
more closely; then he takes a few steps to the open window and holds the bowl in the strong sun light.

                              (CONTINUED)

74   (CONTINUED)

                    WATKINS
          Whatever the nature of this dust
          50,000 years ago, it must have been
          placed in that container for a
          reason...

75   REVERSE ANGLE - THROUGH WINDOW - OVERLAPPING

In the f.g. Watkins is holding up the glass bow; Bryan and Art stand on one side of him; all are looking at the dust in the bowl with awe; in the b.g. can be seen the door; next to it stands the big fan.

                    WATKINS
          We'll spare no effort in finding
          out what that reason was...

The door in the b.g. opens and Tim comes breezing into the laboratory.

                    TIM
               (cheerfully)
          Hi, you test tube roughnecks!..
          Suffering cathead, it's like a
          boiler shed in here!

With a flip of his huge hand Tim turns on the big electric fan! Bryan turns...

                    ART
               (sharply)
          Tim!..Don't!...

But it is too late; with an instant surge the fan has sprung to life - and a gust of air envelops the scientists at the window.

76   CLOSE SHOT - SHALLOW BOWL IN WATKINS' HANDS

The gust of air instantly blows the fine, black dust out of the bowl.

77   WIDER ANGLE

Startled Professor Watkins jerks up his hand to shield the precious dust in the bowl from the draft - but he is too late...The dust from space is blown out the window and swept away by the wind.

                              (CONTINUED)

77   (CONTINUED)

>   ART
>   Tim! The fan! Turn it off!!

Tim - taken aback - turns off the fan.

>   TIM
>   (bewildered)
>   What's wrong?

Watkins turns on him; he is white-lipped with fury; he speaks with seething, quiet rage as he advances upon the stunned Tim...

>   WATKINS
>   Wrong! You idiot! Your <u>blunder</u>
>   just robbed us of the chance of a
>   lifetime! Wrong, you ask! Get out!
>   Get out before I....

>   TIM
>   (scowling)
>   Now, wait just a bit!..I'm sorry,
>   if I...

>   WATKINS
>   (vehemently)
>   Get out!

Art steps between them.

>   ART
>   Tim...You'd better leave...

Watkins turns on his heels and stalks away.

>   ART
>   (quietly; to Tim)
>   I'll talk to you later tonight...
>   At my place...Diane's meeting me
>   there...

Tim glares after Watkins; then he looks at Art; without a word he strides out of the room; Art frowns after him.

78   CLOSEUP - BRYAN

He looks serious; concerned.

79   THREE SHOT

Art looks angrily contemptuous; he scowls after the departing Tim; then he turns to Professor Watkins.

(CONTINUED)

79   (CONTINUED)

                    ART
          Professor Watkins - What can I
          say? I'm sorry! It may be small
          consolation...

80   CLOSEUP - ART - OVERLAPPING

                    ART
          ...but, I'll have to put up with
          that - clumsy oaf - the rest of
          my life!

                                        DISSOLVE:

81   EXT. FRONT ENTRANCE TO SCIENCE BUILDING - NIGHT - MED. LONG SHOT

     The light is on in the hall; it is turned off; a man comes out of the building - locks the door behind him and starts down the steps; it is Bryan.

     It is a beautiful, moonlit night; Bryan walks towards Camera to a MED. SHOT. He stops and looks up at the starry sky with pleasure; as he is watching the stars, the sounds of approaching footsteps can be heard; he looks in their direction.

82   WIDER ANGLE

     Diane comes walking down the path towards Bryan; she stops as Bryan says:

                    BRYAN
          Good evening!..

                    DIANE
          Hi!..Isn't it a beautiful night?

83   TWO SHOT

     Bryan is obviously glad to have run into the girl.

                    BRYAN
          Certainly is...This is the time of
          year I like the campus best -
          summer vacation...when there's
          no one around!...

                                        (CONTINUED)

83   (CONTINUED)

>   DIANE
>   It's so nice and peaceful...
>
>   BRYAN
>   Yes...it is...

The conversation lags a bit awkwardly.

>   DIANE
>   You've been working late...
>
>   BRYAN
>   (with a boyish grin)
>   It's usually the junior partner
>   that's left to do the clean-up
>   jobs!..
>
>   DIANE
>   (with a little
>   laugh)
>   I guess it is...

She starts to leave.

>   BRYAN
>   Wait!..Look...eh...Miss Hawkes...
>
>   DIANE
>   Diane...
>
>   BRYAN
>   And I'm Bryan...Look...I was just
>   on my way to the village for a...
>   a cup of coffee...and I...eh...
>   (he is having
>   trouble asking)
>   I was wondering...eh...
>
>   DIANE
>   (with studied
>   innocence)
>   Yes - Bryan?...
>
>   BRYAN
>   (with a burst
>   of courage)
>   I was wondering if you'd join me?
>
>   DIANE
>   (she is all in
>   favor of the
>   suggestion)
>   Well - I <u>was</u> supposed to meet Dad...
>   and Art...

(CONTINUED)

83   (CONTINUED - 2)

                    BRYAN
              (hastily, taking
              her mention of Tim
              and Art as a polite
              refusal)
          Oh, well...

There is a sudden, sharp clang of metal hitting metal coming from around the corner of the Science Building.

                    DIANE
          What was that?

                    BRYAN
              (frowning)
          I don't know...

He takes the interruption as a welcome excuse to get out of the situation.

                    BRYAN
          I'd better check...
              (he starts away)
          Good night, Diane...See you!...

                    DIANE
              (she was just about
              to accept his in-
              vitation)
          Yes...but...I...

But, it is too late; Bryan is already running silently towards the building corner; Diane looks after him with disappointment; then she continues on her way.

84   MED. SHOT - CORNER

Bryan arrives at the corner; he stops in the shadow hidden from view.

85   MED. CLOSE SHOT

Slowly Bryan peers around the corner; CAMERA TRUCKS with him to see what he sees: About thirty feet away there is a little side door leading into the building; as Bryan watches it is being silently closed - from the inside! Quietly Bryan runs to the door.

86 MED. CLOSE SHOT

Bryan arrives at the door; he sees that the lock has been forced; resolutely he starts to enter the building.

87 INT. CORRIDOR - NIGHT - MED. SHOT - SIDE DOOR

Bryan enters cautiously through the door; he stands for a moment silently - peering into the semi-gloom.

88 ANGLE ACROSS BRYAN DOWN THE CORRIDOR

Half way down the corridor a stair case leads to the upper floors; Bryan (and Camera) can just make out a furtive shadow disappearing up the stairs...Silently Bryan runs to the stair well and stops to listen.

89 CLOSEUP - BRYAN

He is listening intently; faintly we hear hurried footsteps disappearing up the stairs; presently Bryan slowly follows.

90 MED. SHOT - STAIRS

Bryan is slowly mounting the steps; from above we can hear the faint noises made by the intruder...Bryan stops - leans out and looks up the well...

91 ANGLE ACROSS BRYAN UP THROUGH STAIR WELL

The shadows made by the bright moonlight streaming in through the windows create a weirdly alien yet beautiful picture; a moving shadow almost at the third floor level can be seen steadily climbing - to disappear on the third floor landing...Bryan starts in pursuit...

92 INT. THIRD FLOOR CORRIDOR - NIGHT - MED. SHOT

Bryan arrives from the stairs; he keeps to the shadow along the wall; he stops and peers ahead down the corridor.

93 LONG SHOT - CORRIDOR - BRYAN'S P.O.V.

Half way down the corridor the dark figure of a man with his back towards Bryan (Camera) is absorbed in an attempt to break open the lock on a door; it is the door to Laboratory B!

(CONTINUED)

93   (CONTINUED)

Slowly CAMERA DOLLIES IN - closer and closer to the unaware intruder...until the man is seen in a MED. CLOSEUP - still with his back to the Camera...

Suddenly the man turns; his lips instantly draw back in a vicious snarl, his eyes gleam with a fanatic hate, and without warning he leaps at Bryan (Camera) - a long wickedly gleaming screwdriver held high for attack!

94   MED. SHOT

Bryan manages to ward off the stranger's first violent attack, and the two men struggle desperately with each other.

95   THE FIGHT

The fight will be routined; it is a surprisingly vicious one; the intruder fights silently and grimly with a fanatic singleness of purpose: To destroy Bryan! Alarm and fear crowd in upon the young scientist as he finds himself fighting for his life...Finally a punch thrown by Bryan catches the intruder off balance; he falls - cracks his head against the door post - and blacks out...

96   CLOSEUP - BRYAN

He is breathing hard; he looks down upon his unconscious adversary with a mixture of fear, anger and bewilderment; he brushes his hair back from his forehead.

97   MED. SHOT

Bryan unlocks the door to the lab; opens it and switches on the light; in the b.g. the gleaming, black object from space can be seen; Bryan steps through the door into the lab; CAMERA FOLLOWS him; he picks up the phone and dials as CAMERA DOLLIES IN to a CLOSEUP.

            BRYAN
         (on phone)
    Professor Watkins?...could you come
    over to B lab right away!..Someone
    just tried to break in!..Nearly
    killed me!..

                              DISSOLVE:

98   INT. B LABORATORY - NIGHT - MED. SHOT

The intruder is sitting in a chair; Bryan, Watkins and Art are grouped around him; in the b.g. near the door stands the Night Watchman, Bernie, a small, nearsighted gentleman in his sixties; Bernie served in both World Wars and retains many little military mannerisms; Bryan is loosening the intruder's shirt collar; the man moans softly; he is coming to...

Suddenly consciousness seems to rush over him like a flood; he starts - looks around quickly and wildly at the men confronting him; then sits back in the chair, scowling sullenly.

     BRYAN
    (sharply)
  Who are you? What are you doing
  here?

The man makes no answer.

     WATKINS
    (annoyed)
  What were you after? Speak up, man!

The stranger remains silent; he <u>scratches his chest</u>.

     ART
    (grimly)
  Maybe I can make him talk!

     BRYAN
    (to the intruder)
  We'll have to turn you over to the
  police...You understand that?

Still no answer.

     BRYAN
  It might be easier if you'd co-
  operate...

The man merely glares at him.

     BRYAN
  What did you want in this laboratory?
  Did someone send you here?

Suddenly - without the slightest warning - the intruder jumps out of the chair; he laps upon Art...

32.

99 CLOSE TWO SHOT

The stranger rakes his fingernails across Art's cheek, leaving long, ugly gashes; then he leaps away from him.

100 MED. SHOT

The man turns towards the door; Bryan calls sharply to the Night Watchman:

           BRYAN
   Bernie! Watch him!...

The Watchman quickly steps into the doorway; the intruder - hardly glancing at him - without a break in his stride, rushes towards the closed window - and hurls himself head first through the glass panes, crashing and splintering about him, as he tumbles out - and down! The men are stunned; they look in horror at the empty, demolished window.

           WATKINS
      (in a half-whisper)
   My God! Three stories...

Bryan runs for the door.

           BRYAN
   Come on!!...

The others follow.

101 EXT. - NIGHT - MED. LONG SHOT ACROSS BODY OF INTRUDER IN F.G. TO FRONT ENTRANCE OF SCIENCE BUILDING

The body of the man lies completely still - in a grotesquely unnatural position; Bryan comes running out of the building towards the still figure; the others follow him closely.

102 ANOTHER ANGLE

Bryan and the others reach the intruder; Bryan hurriedly yet carefully examines him; then he looks up at the others...

           WATKINS
      (stunned)
   Why? Why did he do it??

                 (CONTINUED)

102   (CONTINUED)

Bryan shakes his head; he looks down upon the man; the stranger's glassy eyes stare back at him - unseeingly.

          BRYAN
We'll never know - now...

103   CLOSE SHOT - THE INTRUDER

In the fall from the window his shirt has been torn open at the chest, where Bryan loosened it; a distinctive, red, streaky rash can be plainly seen on his chest; no one pays any attention to it, as Bryan quietly passes his hand over the dead man's face to close his staring eyes.

104   WIDER SHOT

Bryan stands up; he turns to the Night Watchman.

          BRYAN
Call the sheriff, will you Bernie?

          BERNIE
      (he touches his
      cap)
Yes, Mr. Kenmore...Right away!

He moves towards the building. The others stand looking at the dead intruder.

          DISSOLVE:

105   INT. B LABORATORY - NIGHT - CLOSE SHOT - SHERIFF, MORGAN - PULL BACK

Present are Bryan, Watkins, Art and Bernie; also Sheriff Larry Morgan and at the door Officer Sergeant Strauss. Morgan is slightly pompous, not adverse to a little graft...

From below can be heard the faint sounds of an ambulance door being slammed shut, and the vehicle being started; followed by the howl of a siren starting up and disappearing in the distance, during:

          SHERIFF
...And you have no idea what he was after?

          (CONTINUED)

105 (CONTINUED)

                    WATKINS
We have some valuable equipment here...

                    SHERIFF
I see...

                    ART
It isn't the first time someone's broken in during the summer hiatus.

                    SHERIFF
            (he doesn't under-
            stand the word)
Eh?...Of course...
            (importantly)
But there is nothing missing now?

                    WATKINS
No...

Watkins, standing next to the space object, looks at it and puts his hand on it.

                    WATKINS (cont'd)
...Everything seems to be safe.

                    BRYAN
Professor Watkins...Maybe the thief wasn't after the equipment?

                    WATKINS
What else?

                    BRYAN
            (indicating the
            object)
That!

                    WATKINS
            (startled)
But - nobody knows about it - except us!

                    ART
And the drilling crew!

Watkins reacts.

                    WATKINS
You could be right...

                                    (CONTINUED)

105 (CONTINUED - 2)

                SHERIFF
            (with curiosity)
What is it?

                ART
As a matter of fact, Sheriff, we aren't quite sure yet...

                WATKINS
It was found deep in the earth...

                ART
It could turn out to be a valuable discovery....

                SHERIFF
            (with new interest)
Yeah? You mean - like an archeological find...To put in a museum?

                ART
Something like that...

                SHERIFF
You don't say! Could be what that fellow was after, all right...

                ART
Yes...So you can understand, Sheriff, why we would like to be able to complete our work undisturbed...

                SHERIFF
Of course...

                ART
If we are successful it might be very rewarding for us...And for anyone who helped us!

He looks meaningfully at the Sheriff.

                SHERIFF
            (he takes the bait;
            his greediness is
            showing)
I see...
            (officiously)
Who lives out here at the moment... On the campus, I mean?

                          (CONTINUED)

105 (CONTINUED - 3)

> WATKINS
> We do.

> BRYAN
> There's the janitor, Hans Jensen...Fanny, the cleaning woman...and the gardener - Sammy...

> SHERIFF
> Anyone else?

> WATKINS
> No. The University is closed for the summer...I use this time every year to do some research...

> SHERIFF
> Tell you what I'll do...Tomorrow I'll send Sergeant Strauss, there, and another man out here...They can stay on for the next few days...You won't have any more trouble...

> ART
> Thank you very much, Sheriff...We appreciate that...

> SHERIFF
> Glad to do it!
> (he turns to Watkins)
> Have you got a gun?

> WATKINS
> (indignantly)
> Now, what would I be doing with a gun!?

> SHERIFF
> (to Sergeant Strauss)
> Let me have yours, Sol...

Strauss gives the Sheriff his service revolver; the Sheriff hands it to Watkins.

> SHERIFF
> Here...Better hang on to this...

Watkins takes the gun with obvious distaste, and drops it in a desk drawer; the Sheriff starts to leave, during:

(CONTINUED)

105   (CONTINUED - 4)

                    SHERIFF
          Close and lock the gate down there
          - and you'll be all right for to-
          night...
                (he turns at the door)
          You know, I work quite a bit with
          science myself...Our modern crime
          detection methods are very scien-
          tific...Yes, Sir, very!..Good night!

He closes the door to their chorused 'good nights'.

106   CLOSER ANGLE

                    WATKINS
          Fatuous ass!

                    ART
                (he grins)
          But he did promise us protection!

                    WATKINS
          I just hope it isn't too late...
                (he goes to the
                 object)
          Bryan. That madman never did get
          in here, did he?

                    BRYAN
          No...Not until we brought him in
          ourselves.

Watkins has been examining the electro-magnetic set-up.

                    WATKINS
          Hmmm - Looks all right...

He tries out a couple of connections; moves the helix
back and forth - leaving it under the end of the object
which does not show the opening!

                    WATKINS
          Just in case - let's try the equip-
          ment...Bryan - turn on the current.

Bryan moves to obey; the whine as before gets higher
and higher...

107   CLOSE SHOT - OBJECT

The whine reaches its peak; nothing happens...

108 MED. SHOT

                    ART
        Seems to work perfectly...

                    WATKINS
        Yes...You can turn it off, Bryan...

                    BRYAN
        Let me try something...

He goes to the object and adjusts the helix under the back end of the spheroid so it is at exactly right angles to its axis; then he stands back and looks at it; the whine is the only sound heard...

109 CLOSE GROUP SHOT

The three men are watching the object; Watkins is just about to make a remark to Bryan, when Art points to the object.

                    ART
        Look!..

On the side towards the men another circular area the same size as the first begins to grow lighter and lighter...CAMERA DOLLIES in to a CLOSE SHOT of the OBJECT as the disc slowly rotates, screwing itself outwards, and finally swivels aside to hang from the rim of a second opening into the space object!

110 CLOSE GROUP SHOT

Bryan shines a flashlight into the opening; he looks into it.

                    BRYAN
        Looks just like the other one...
        And - there's more dust on the
        bottom!..About the same amount as
        before...

CAMERA DOLLIES in quickly to fill the screen with a CLOSEUP of the round opening; the flashlight beam reveals a handful of dark dust lying on the bottom of the small compartment...

                                        DISSOLVE:

111   INT. WATKINS' OFFICE - NIGHT - CLOSE SHOT - WALL SAFE

The screen is filled with the round opening of a small wall safe; in it stands a glass laboratory bottle half filled with the dark space dust; CAMERA DOLLIES out to a MED. THREE SHOT of Watkins, Bryan and Art...

The office is nicely and comfortably furnished and appointed; it is on the ground floor facing the gateway; several touches mark it as the study of a scientist and administrator.

Watkins closes the safe door - and swings a picture of Heatherton University in front of it, during:

> WATKINS
> We'll take no chances this time...
> We'll keep the dust in the safe -
> except for the minute, specific
> quantities we need for our studies...

He walks to the window and looks out into the night.

> WATKINS
> Bryan...

> BRYAN
> Yes, Professor?

Watkins turns to him.

> WATKINS
> I would like you to stay here to-
> night - in my office...You can sleep
> on the couch...do you mind?

> BRYAN
> Not at all.

> WATKINS
> Thank you...I'd feel much better...

He looks out the window again.

> WATKINS
> Tomorrow the Sheriff's men will be
> here...

112   EXT. GATEWAY - NIGHT - LONG SHOT - WATKINS' P.O.V.
       OVERLAPPING

The gate is closed; Bernie can be seen trying the lock; suddenly he slaps his neck to kill a mosquito (plant for later sequence) - then he moves on...

(CONTINUED)

112   (CONTINUED)

                    WATKINS (O.S.)
               ...then I hope we can work in peace!

                                             DISSOLVE:

113   INT. WATKINS' OFFICE - NIGHT - PAN SHOT

      CAMERA SLOWLY PANS the room until it comes to rest on a
      MED. CLOSEUP of Bryan; he is lying on the sofa; he is
      asleep.

114   WIDER ANGLE

      Suddenly the beam from a flashlight shines through the
      window from the outside; it wanders aimlessly across
      the dark room.

115   CLOSE SHOT - BRYAN

      The flashlight beam cuts across his face - and moves
      on, out of the shot...suddenly Bryan sits up with a
      start...

116   WIDER ANGLE

      Bryan looks around; something disturbed him: What?...
      The flashlight beam has disappeared.

117   CLOSE SHOT - BRYAN

      He is listening intently; there is utter silence, ex-
      cept for the faint sounds of the crickets coming from
      outside the window...Bryan looks thoughtful; quietly
      he stands up - and CAMERA FOLLOWS him as he walks to
      the door - and goes out.

118   EXT. OUTSIDE WINDOW TO WATKINS' OFFICE - NIGHT -
      MED. SHOT

      Bryan comes into the picture; he looks around cautiously;
      he walks close to the windows; he looks around search-
      ingly...Suddenly he spots something on the ground; he
      kneels to inspect it.

119   CLOSE SHOT

Bryan is kneeling; he is examining a deep footprint in the soft earth beneath the window...Suddenly a hand holding a large revolver comes into the picture; Bryan is startled by the sound of a hoarse whisper...

>   VOICE (O.S.)
>   (in a gruff whisper)
>   Don't move, Mister!

Bryan freezes.

>   VOICE (O.S.)
>   Stand up!

Bryan obeys.

>   VOICE (O.S.)
>   Put your hands back of your neck...
>   turn around!..

Bryan starts to turn...

120   CLOSE SHOT - BRYAN

He is turning towards his unseen capturer (Camera); as he faces him, a strong flashlight beam hits him full in the face, making him squint.

>   VOICE (O.S.)
>   (with surprise)
>   Mr. Kenmore!

The flashlight goes out.

121   TWO SHOT - OVERLAPPING

>   VOICE
>   It's me!..Bernie!..I thought you
>   were another burglar!
>
>   BRYAN
>   Somebody was out here...
>
>   VOICE
>   Nobody around but me...
>
>   BRYAN
>   (he grins)
>   I'd better stop seeing dragons in
>   the sky!...
>   (continued)

(CONTINUED)

121   (CONTINUED)

                    BRYAN (cont'd)
               (he starts off)
          Good night, Bernie...

                    BERNIE
          Good night, Mr. Kenmore...See you
          in the morning...

                                        DISSOLVE:

122   EXT. GATEWAY - DAY - LONG SHOT - BUILDING P.O.V.

       It is morning; the gate is open; near the gate a man is
       working peacefully in a flower bed; it is Sammy Tokuzo,
       the gardener, a small Japanese of about 35; no one can
       be seen at the gate - then two police officers come
       walking into view from outside; they are Sergeant Strauss
       and Officer Lawson; they take up positions at the gate.

123   INT. B LABORATORY - DAY - MED. SHOT

       Watkins is sitting at a table; Art and Bryan stand
       behind him; the Professor is looking through a micro-
       scope; in the b.g. the object from space can be seen.

                    WATKINS
          You're right, Bryan...It isn't
          just ordinary dust...The particles
          are too regular...

                    BRYAN
               (with interest)
          What do you make of it?...

                    WATKINS
          I can't say. Not without extensive
          research and experiments...

                    ART
               (he indicates the
                space object)
          What about the container, itself?
          I think we should concentrate on
          the tests that we already...

                    WATKINS
               (interrupting)
          You and I will make them. Bryan,
          you run the preliminary analysis
          on the dust...that's more in your
          line...

                                        (CONTINUED)

123   (CONTINUED)

                    BRYAN
               (enthusiastically)
          Yes, Sir!

                    WATKINS
          ...make the obvious eliminations...
          classify any elements present...It
          may have no importance - but see
          what you can find out...

                    BRYAN
          I'll get right on it!

                    WATKINS
          Good. Dr. Corliss and I will be
          busy with that infernal 'thing'...
               (he nods at the object)
          the rest of the day...

                                   DISSOLVE:

124   EXT. GATEWAY - NIGHT - OFFICE P.O.V.

      The gate is closed; Sergeant Strauss and Officer Lawson
      can be seen guarding it; the moon is out - it is a peace-
      ful night, the silence of which is disturbed only by the
      chirping of the crickets and the song of a mockingbird...
      Sergeant Strauss lazily slaps at a mosquito...

125   INT. WATKINS' OFFICE - NIGHT - MED. SHOT

      Watkins, Bryan and Art are finishing up the day's work;
      Bryan is typing up some reports; Art is filing slides;
      Watkins is writing; he gets up and hands a sheet of
      paper to Bryan.

                    WATKINS
          That's the last one...You can do it
          tomorrow...

                    BRYAN
          I'd just as soon finish up tonight.

                    ART
          A full day's work - and no results!

                    WATKINS
               (pointedly)
          There'll be a lot more work, Dr.
          Corliss, before we have our
          answers!

                                   (CONTINUED)

125   (CONTINUED)

Suddenly there is a faint, thudding sound from the corridor outside the door.

>   WATKINS
>   What was that?

>   BRYAN
>   (suddenly alert)
>   Quiet!

Watkins looks at him with surprise; there is a sudden knock on the door; the men look questioningly at each other; Bryan runs silently to the window; he looks out.

>   BRYAN
>   The guards are on the gate...

>   ART
>   And Bernie is watching the front...

>   WATKINS
>   Then who...?

The knock is repeated; Bryan runs to the door; he flattens himself against the wall; he nods to Art.

>   ART
>   (with an uncertain
>   look at Watkins)
>   Come - in!..

Slowly the door opens - and a man cautiously sticks his head in; it is Tim; he looks sheepish.

>   ART
>   Tim! What are you doing here?

>   TIM
>   Is it all right to come in?

>   ART
>   Of course. Come in...

Tim enters, followed by Diane; Bryan and Diane see each other.

126   TWO SHOT - BRYAN AND DIANE

They smile at one another.

127   WIDER ANGLE - GROUP

> ART
> Hello, Dee...

> DIANE
> Good evening, Art...Professor Watkins...

Watkins is not pleased at the sight of Tim; he merely grunts.

> ART
> What are you doing here?

Tim takes out some papers and hands them to Art.

> TIM
> I've got the dope you wanted - on the drill bits...Thought I'd bring it over...

> ART
> Fine. Thanks a lot...

Tim is obviously ill at ease.

> TIM
> Look...eh...I want you all to know how sorry I am...for causing that trouble...when I barged in the other day...

> ART
> Forget it...

Suddenly there is a shot from outside; then two more.

> BRYAN
> Shots! Somebody's shooting!..

Everyone rushes to the windows.

128   EXT. GATEWAY - NIGHT   LONG SHOT - OFFICE P.O.V.

The iron grill gate is closed; Sergeant Strauss and Officer Lawson can be seen crouched on either side behind the stone gate pillars; they fare firing around the posts at a small truck, which comes careening towards the closed gate - its headlights full on, its motor roaring; without slowing down the truck crashes through the gate and comes to a screeching stop in the driveway before the front entrance to the building; a handful of men jump out - firing as they do.

129   INT. WATKINS' OFFICE - NIGHT - MED. SHOT

For a brief moment everyone seems thunderstruck; a bullet comes crashing through the window and buries itself in the wall; Bryan looks to Professor Watkins; the Professor looks completely bewildered - utterly unable to cope with the situation.

>   BRYAN
> Professor?
>
>   WATKINS
> What - what are we going to do?...

Bryan looks towards Art.

130   CLOSE SHOT - ART

He is standing with his back to the wall near the window; he looks white-lipped and frightened.

131   MED. SHOT

Another shot whizzes through the shattered window; a picture on the wall crashes in a myriad splinters. Suddenly Bryan springs into action; he leaps for the light switch; turns off the lights; the shooting outside intensifies.

>   BRYAN
> Get down! Everybody!
>   (he turns to Watkins)
> Where's the gun?
>
>   WATKINS
> Wha - What gun?
>
>   BRYAN
> The Sheriff's!
>
>   WATKINS
> In the desk.
>
>   BRYAN
> Get it.
>
>   WATKINS
> What! But...
>
>   BRYAN
>   (with unsuspected
>   command)
> <u>Get it!</u>

(CONTINUED)

131 (CONTINUED)

Stunned Watkins obeys.

     BRYAN
     (to Art)
 You stay here...Take care of Diane
 ...Keep down!

He grabs the gun Watkins is taking out of the desk and runs for the door.

     TIM

 Bryan!..

Bryan doesn't slow down, he starts out the door.

     BRYAN

 Come on, Tim!

He runs out the door followed by Tim.

132 EXT. AREA IN FRONT OF SCIENCE BUILDING - LONG SHOT

The truck is standing in front of the entrance; three men are firing from the cover of its wheels at Strauss and Lawson at the gateway; the officers are returning the fire; four other men are trying to make their way to the front entrance to the building.

133 CLOSE SHOT - TRUCK

The men are firing.

134 CLOSE SHOT - STRAUSS

He is crouched behind the stone gate post; he is firing grimly.

135 MED. SHOT - FRONT STEPS

The four men are steadily getting closer to the door taking advantage of whatever cover they can find; from a small window next to the door someone is firing at them.

136 INT. HALL AT FRONT ENTRANCE - NIGHT - MED. SHOT

Bernie is crouched at a small window at the side of the door; he shoots with his revolver through a broken pane;

(CONTINUED)

136   (CONTINUED)

on the other side of the door stands Sammy; he is clad in gaudy pajamas; he holds a garden pickax in his hands; he looks scared, mad and frustrated all at the same time; Bryan and Tim come running into the picture; Bernie looks back and sees them.

> BERNIE
> (calling over the noise)
> Take the other window!

Bryan at once takes up position at the little window on the other side of the door and begins to fire through it at the attackers.

137   EXT. FRONT STEPS - NIGHT - BRYAN'S P.O.V.

The men are advancing; suddenly one of them is hit; he spins around and falls to the ground lifeless; the others retreat a little and take cover - firing all the time.

138   ANOTHER ANGLE - ACROSS MEN TO BUILDING CORNER

The remaining three attackers on the steps are firing at the front door; in the b.g. around the corner of the building comes the janitor, Hans Jensen; he is trying to shrug his pants suspenders over his shoulders as he runs; one of the men sees him; he turns and raises his rifle - taking aim...

139   SHOT ACROSS MAN AND RIFLE TO THE RUNNING JENSEN

Suddenly the rifle belches flame and smoke and sound; Jensen clutches his shoulder and falls to the ground.

140   INT. HALL - NIGHT - CLOSE SHOT - BRYAN

He shoots through the little window.

141   EXT. - NIGHT - CLOSE SHOT - MAN WHO SHOT JENSEN

He suddenly grabs his leg; his rifle clatters to the ground, as he falls on his side.

49 WIDER ANGLE - AREA

The two remaining men from the attack on the front door retreat towards the truck; one of the men shooting from behind a wheel is hit and slumps to the ground; suddenly the remaining four attackers sprint for the truck; jump in and take off at breakneck speed through the demolished gate down the road...

The shooting stops...The silence is shattering...

143 ANGLE ON FRONT DOOR

It is slowly being opened; Bryan comes out followed by Tim, Bernie and Sammy; they walk down to the dead attacker on the steps.

144 CLOSER ANGLE

The men are gathered around the body.

                BRYAN
        Bernie...You and Sammy take care
        of the other one...

                BERNIE
        Right!

He and Sammy run off; CAMERA DOLLIES in to a TWO SHOT.

                TIM
        What's going on, Bryan? What's
        going on??

                BRYAN
           (almost incredulously)
        It was an attack. A <u>planned</u>, <u>organ-</u>
        <u>ized attack</u>!

                TIM
        But - why???

145 WIDER ANGLE - STEPS

Bryan shrugs worriedly; he kneels at the dead attacker's side. Watkins, Art and Diane come hurrhing down the steps to him; Diane rushes up to Bryan.

                DIANE
        Are you all right?

                (CONTINUED)

145   (CONTINUED)

                    BRYAN
            I'm all right...

    He is looking closely at the dead man; Tim puts his arm
    around his daughter; Bryan suddenly turns to Art.

                    BRYAN
            Art. You remember the man a few
            days ago...the burglar...

146   CLOSEUP - BRYAN - OVERLAPPING

                    BRYAN
            ...The one that jumped through the
            window?

147   CLOSEUP - ART

    He frowns.

                    ART
            Yes.

148   CLOSE SHOT - BRYAN

                    BRYAN
            Do you recall anything odd about
            him? Anything special?

149   CLOSE SHOT - ART

                    ART
            No-o...

                    BRYAN (O.S.)
                    (insistently)
            When we found him - right here?

                    ART
            I don't...wait!...Yes...he had
            some marks...some sort of rash -
            on his chest...

150   CLOSE SHOT - BRYAN - OVERLAPPING

                    ART
            ...Is that what you mean?

                                        (CONTINUED)

150   (CONTINUED)

                    BRYAN
          That's what I mean!

He turns to the body; CAMERA PANS quickly to a CLOSE
SHOT of the dead man; Bryan pulls away his open shirt;
on his chest is the identical red, streaky rash that
the first intruder displayed.

                    BRYAN (O.S.)
          Look!

                    ART (O.S.)
          The rash! He has it too!

151   WIDER GROUP SHOT

                    BRYAN
                  (thoughtfully)
          That burglar wasn't alone!..

                    DIANE
                  (frightened)
          What does it mean?

                    BRYAN
                  (troubled)
          I - don't know...

Strauss and Lawson are joining the group with the
wounded attacker from the truck.

152   THREE SHOT - STRAUSS, LAWSON, PRISONER

They are walking towards the group on the steps.

                    STRAUSS
          Go call Morgan. I'll handle this
          fellow.

                    LAWSON
          Okay...

They reach the group.

153   WIDER ANGLE - GROUP

Lawson continues on into the building, during:

                                        (CONTINUED)

153   (CONTINUED)

                    STRAUSS
          Here's one of them, Professor
          Watkins. We winged this one.

                    WATKINS
          Yes...yes...I don't understand...
          How can a thing like this happen...
          In a civilized community! It's
          outrageous!...

Bernie and Sammy come over with the other attacker who
was hit; they are followed by Jensen, who is holding
his injured shoulder. (During the following Diane makes
a temporary bandage for Jensen's wound and puts his arm
in a kerchief sling, in the b.g.)

Bryan grimly goes up to the man held by Strauss; without any preliminaries he rips open his shirt...

154   TWO SHOT - BRYAN, STRANGER

The rash covers the man's chest!

                    BRYAN
                 (sharply)
          Who are you? What are you after?

The man glares at him sullenly, but makes no reply; he
scratches his chest.

                    BRYAN
          What were you trying to do? What
          do you want?

155   WIDER ANGLE

                    STRAUSS
          You're wasting your breath. That
          guy won't open his mouth.

Abruptly Bryan turns on the other captive; the man suddenly makes a move to break away, but Bernie and Sammy
hold him; Bryan tears open his shirt; he, too, has the
strange rash! The onlookers gasp; they look at the man
with a mixture of horror and revulsion. Lawson returns
from the building and talks to Sergeant Strauss, during:

                    BRYAN
          All of them!..They've all got the
          same infection!
                    (continued)

                                        (CONTINUED)

155 (CONTINUED)

> BRYAN (cont'd)
> (he turns to Watkins)
> Professor Watkins. I don't know what all this means...But could it, in some strange way, be connected with that - 'thing' - from space?

> WATKINS
> I don't know, Bryan...Maybe...

> ART
> But _how_? What could it be...?

Strauss walks up to them.

> STRAUSS
> Lawson, here, just talked to the Sheriff...

> ART
> What did he say?

> STRAUSS
> He wants us to bring the prisoners in right away...He wants everyone else to stay here...

> ART
> But - you can't leave us alone!..

> STRAUSS
> Sorry - that's the Sheriff's orders... You'll be okay for a couple of hours... We'll be back by then with more men... Sheriff's rounding up some deputies now...

> DIANE
> You'd better take Mr. Jensen with you, Sergeant. He needs medical attention too...

> STRAUSS
> Will do, Miss.

The two wounded prisoners are herded into the back of the squad car by Lawson, who climbs in with them; Jensen gets into the front of the car, during:

> WATKINS
> You _will_ be back...I don't understand all _this_...I hope the Sheriff can find out...

(CONTINUED)

155   (CONTINUED - 2)

                    STRAUSS
            Morgan's a good man...He'll find
            out...

He turns to get into the car.

                    BRYAN
            One thing, Sergeant...

                    STRAUSS
            What is it, young fellow?

                    BRYAN
            Your guns. Leave us your rifles...
            Just in case..!

                    STRAUSS
            Sure thing!

He hands Bryan and Tim his and Lawson's rifles, taking
out his revolver instead; during:

                    STRAUSS
                (to Bryan; with a
                 friendly grin)
            And if I were you - I'd park a car
            across that there gate - after
            we're out of here...also - just in
            case!

Strauss gets into the car; he leans out of the window:

                    STRAUSS
            We'll be back within two hours...

The car starts up...

                                        DISSOLVE:

156   EXT. CAMPUS - SUNRISE - SCENIC LONG SHOT

      It is a beautiful shot; the sun is rising majestically
      on the horizon.

157   INT. WATKINS' OFFICE - DAY - CLOSE SHOT TELEPHONE AND
      PULL BACK TO MED. SHOT

      A hand is jiggling the phone; CAMERA PULLS BACK to re-
      veal Art impatiently trying to get the telephone
      operator to answer; grouped around him are Watkins,

                                        (CONTINUED)

157 (CONTINUED)

Tim and Diane; Bryan stands at the window looking out; everyone looks worried.

> ART
> (on phone)
> Operator!..Operator!...
> (he hangs up)
> It's no use...I can't get through...

> DIANE
> Is the phone all right?

> ART
> Seems to be...Only I can't get the operator to answer...

> WATKINS
> It's daylight already...The Sheriff should have been here hours ago...

> ART
> Now we can't even get him on the phone!

> WATKINS
> What do you think we should do, Bryan?

Art reacts to the fact that Watkins turns to Bryan instead of him.

158 MED. CLOSEUP - BRYAN

> BRYAN
> Staying around here - waiting - is no good...

He looks out the window.

159 EXT. GATEWAY - DAY - OFFICE P.O.V. - OVERLAPPING

A car is parked on the drive directly across the gateway with the broken gate, blocking the entrance effectively; Bernie and Sammy can be seen guarding it with rifles.

> BRYAN (O.S.)
> Looks pretty peaceful out there...

160 INT. WATKINS' OFFICE - DAY - MED. CLOSEUP - BRYAN - OVERLAPPING

As he talks he walks to the others; CAMERA CARRIES him to a MED. GROUP SHOT.

> BRYAN
> The best thing would be for one of us to go down to the Sheriff's Office and find out what's up... I'll do it...

> ART
> (maliciously)
> You've got all the answers, haven't you, Kenmore?...

> BRYAN
> (surprised)
> I just want to get to the bottom of this...

> WATKINS
> That's enough, Dr. Corliss! Bryan seems to know what he's doing...

Art scowls; his jealousy is beginning to show.

> TIM
> Want me along, Bryan?

> BRYAN
> Better stay here.

> DIANE
> (genuinely concerned)
> Be careful! You don't know **what's** happened!

> ART
> (he reacts to Diane's attitude)
> You don't have to worry about **him**, Dee...The danger spot is here!

He gives Bryan a sharp glance; then looks back at Diane - musingly.

> BRYAN
> Art's right, Diane...I'll be okay...
> (he turns to Watkins)
> I'll be back as soon as I can...

(CONTINUED)

160   (CONTINUED)

                    WATKINS
          Good! I want to know what that
          lunatic Sheriff thinks he's doing!..

                    BRYAN
          I'll take the jeep....

He starts for the door; Diane looks after him...

                              DISSOLVE:

161   EXT. ROAD - DAY - LONG SHOT

A jeep comes speeding along the road, past camera (which PANS with it) and on...

162   EXT. SMALL TOWN STREET - DAY - LONG SHOT

It appears to be a typical, friendly, lazy small community; several people go about their business - enjoying the fine, sunny day; in the b.g. a jeep comes into view; it is being driven by Bryan.

163   CLOSE SHOT - BRYAN

He is driving along slowly, looking around.

164   SIDEWALK - SHOT FROM SLOWLY MOVING JEEP - BRYAN'S P.O.V.

A little girl is skipping rope on the sidewalk; she collides with a couple of men standing at the curb talking; she looks up at them - startled; they smile at her; one of them reaches down and tousles her hair, and she skips on.

165   ANOTHER ANGLE - AS ABOVE

The jeep is passing a barber shop; the barber is just taking leave of a customer in the open door; they part; another man passes by the barber; the barber greets him with a friendly gesture; the man ignores him completely; the barber looks puzzled; suddenly the man - oblivious to everything - cuts across the street directly in front of the jeep, causing Bryan to jam on the brakes.

58.

166   MED. LONG SHOT - STREET

Bryan, in the jeep, has come to a stop in order to avoid hitting the careless pedestrian; he looks after the man as the latter blithely continues on his way; then Bryan starts up again.

167   MED. LONG SHOT - STREET IN FRONT OF SHERIFF'S OFFICE

Bryan brings his jeep to a halt behind two police motorcycles which are parked at the curb in front of the Sheriff's Office; he jumps from the jeep and proceeds into the building.

168   INT. POLICE STATION ANTE-ROOM - DAY - MED. SHOT

It is a fair sized room; a counter-desk divides it into two parts; there are a couple of desks and several chairs in the office part, and a couple of doors lead out of the room; one of them is marked: LAWRENCE T. MORGAN - SHERIFF. A police officer is standing at the counter-desk looking through some papers; it is Officer Lawson; Bryan enters; he walks up to Lawson.

                  BRYAN
Officer Lawson!

Lawson looks up quickly; his eyes narrow.

                  LAWSON
Oh...It's you.

                  BRYAN
What happened?

                  LAWSON
What do you want?

                  BRYAN
         (he reacts to Lawson's attitude)
Where's the Sheriff?

Lawson glares at him.

                  LAWSON
Wait here.

He goes to the Sheriff's Office and enters.

169 CLOSEUP - BRYAN

He frowns after the officer.

170 MED. SHOT - ACROSS BRYAN TO SHERIFF'S OFFICE DOOR

The door opens and Lawson beckons to Bryan.

> LAWSON
> Sheriff wants to see you.

Bryan walks through the swinging half-door to the office part of the room and enters the Sheriff's Office.

171 INT. SHERIFF'S OFFICE - DAY - MED. SHOT

The office is small and functionally furnished. Sheriff Morgan sits behind his desk; he does not get up; gone is his friendly, harmless pomposity; he looks cold and shrewd. Bryan enters, followed by Lawson, who takes up position at the door behind him.

> SHERIFF
> (pointing to a chair)
> Sit down.

> BRYAN
> Sheriff! We've been trying to get you...

> SHERIFF
> (firmly; coldly)
> Sit - down!

Bryan sits.

> BRYAN
> What's going on? Why didn't you come out??

172 TWO SHOT - OVERLAPPING

> BRYAN
> What happened to the prisoners? Who were they? What were they after??

> SHERIFF
> Suppose you let me ask the questions!

173 CLOSEUP - SHERIFF - OVERLAPPING

>   SHERIFF
> You haven't been attacked again -
> have you?

174 CLOSEUP - BRYAN

>   BRYAN
> No - but...

175 TWO SHOT

>   SHERIFF
> And you won't be...There's no need
> for me to tie up my men out there.

176 CLOSEUP - BRYAN

>   BRYAN
> No need! After all that's happened?
> As long as we don't know how many
> others there are that have that...

He breaks off suddenly; his eyes widen with shock.

177 MED. CLOSEUP - SHERIFF

He is looking with narrowed eyes at Bryan; he is absent-mindedly and unconsciously scratching his chest! CAMERA ZOOMS in to a CLOSE SHOT of the SHERIFF'S HAND...

178 TWO SHOT

>   SHERIFF
> Yes? Go on!

He is unaware of Bryan's observation - and suspicion.

>   BRYAN
>   (desperately trying
>   to control himself;
>   thinking fast and hard)
> That - eh - how many others that
> have the...the intention of -
> attacking us...

He is gradually regaining his composure.

179   TWO SHOT - O.S. SHOT SHERIFF TO BRYAN - OVERLAPPING

                    BRYAN
            ...we need protection...

180   TWO SHOT - O.S. SHOT BRYAN TO SHERIFF

                    SHERIFF
                (with a mirthless
                 grin)
            You do - do you?

181   MED. SHOT

                    BRYAN
            But, I guess you're right, Sheriff...

Morgan nods imperceptibly to Lawson behind Bryan; the officer silently begins to move towards Bryan.

                    BRYAN (cont'd)
            We can protect ourselves, now...
            We took your tip!

Morgan is startled; he quickly stops Lawson with a sharp glance.

                    SHERIFF
            My tip?

                    BRYAN
            Sure...About scientific crime detection! Only we're using scientific crime prevention! Got quite a little surprise rigged up - for our next visitors!

                    SHERIFF
                (shrewdly interested)
            Really? Go on...

                    BRYAN
            Come on back with me - and I'll show you.

                    SHERIFF
                (ominously)
            Tell me about it - now.

                    BRYAN
                (he shrugs)
            All right...It's like this...Wait a moment...

                                (CONTINUED)

181   (CONTINUED)

Morgan and Lawson both tense.

      BRYAN (cont'd)
  I'll show you the <u>plans</u>! I've got
  them in the jeep...
    (he gets up)
  Won't be a minute!..

Lawson, behind Bryan, makes a move to detain him; Morgan stops him with a look; Bryan pretends not to notice the by-play; he walks to the door; Morgan nods to Lawson to follow him; they leave the office.

182   MED. CLOSEUP - MORGAN

He looks after the two men with narrowed eyes and a grim expression; absentmindedly he again scratches his chest.

183   EXT. STREET IN FRONT OF SHERIFF'S OFFICE - DAY - MED. WIDE SHOT

Bryan and Lawson come out of the building and walk to Bryan's jeep.

184   CLOSER ANGLE

Bryan bends over the back of the jeep; a lot of different things can be seen lying there; a two-gallon can of oil; a jack; a few gardening tools; a carton; a canvas bag; etc...Bryan lifts out the oil can and sets it on the floor in front; he rummages among the stuff in the back.

      BRYAN
  Here it is.

Lawson bends closer; without warning Bryan suddenly swings around with both his fists clenched together; he strikes Lawson full in the face with a tremendous blow, which sends the officer sprawling; then he jumps into the jeep...

185   WIDER ANGLE

Morgan comes running from the building; he sprints for the jeep; Bryan has just got it started; he swerves sharply; Morgan misses him, and the jeep roars off down the street, as Morgan sends a couple of wild bullets flying after it...Then he and Lawson, who has picked himself up, race for the two motorcycles parked at the cub; and they screech off in pursuit - sirens wailing...

186   EXT. STREET - DAY - HEAD-ON SHOT - LONG SHOT

Bryan's jeep comes racing down the street; it passes close by Camera; following only a short distance behind Morgan and Lawson roar in pursuit - passing Camera closely on either side.

187   EXT. - DAY - VARIOUS PURSUIT SHOTS

The shots will be selected on location to take advantage of the layout and terrain; it is a fast and furious chase with the two motorcycles in close pursuit of the jeep.

188   EXT. TWO-LANE MACADAM ROAD - DAY - MED. SHOT

Bryan's jeep is roaring down the traffic-free road.

189   MED. CLOSEUP - BRYAN - TRAVEL SHOT

He is intent on getting every ounce of power out of the jeep; he glances at the side rear-view mirror.

190   CLOSE SHOT - REAR-VIEW MIRROR

In it can be seen the two pursuing motorcycles; they seem to be gaining on the clear stretch of the road.

191   CLOSEUP - BRYAN

He looks grim; he glances around - sees the oil can standing on the floor in front next to him; he gets an idea...

192   MED. CLOSE SHOT - FROM LEAD CAMERA CAR TO JEEP - TRAVEL SHOT

Bryan carefully picks up the can with his right hand, while he drives with the left; he unscrews the cap; shifting hands he holds the open can out over the side of the jeep, pouring the oil out on the roadway, while he rapidly swerves the vehicle from one side to the other.

193   WIDER ANGLE - INCLUDING JEEP AND MOTORCYCLES - TRAVEL SHOT

Bryan is finished; the jeep roars on; in the b.g. the two pursuing motorcycles can be seen; they come to the big oil slick made by Bryan on the road; suddenly they begin to skid and slide...

64.

194 ANGLE ON MOTORCYCLES

They are skidding on the oil; the men lose control, and the two motorcycles spin off the road...

195 ANGLE FROM LEAD CAMERA CAR TO JEEP AND MOTORCYCLES - TRAVEL SHOT

Bryan's jeep races down the road; in the far b.g. the two police officers can be seen getting up; they stand on the road and look after the fleeing jeep...

DISSOLVE:

196 EXT. ROAD LEADING TO SCIENCE BUILDING GATEWAY - DAY - LONG SHOT

A jeep is driving fast down the road towards the gateway.

197 CLOSEUP - BRYAN - TRAVEL SHOT

It is Bryan; he is alone; he looks grim.

198 TRAVEL SHOT - BRYAN'S P.O.V.

The jeep is nearing the gateway; across the road in the gateway the car is parked as a roadblock; no one is in sight; the jeep comes to a halt about twenty feet from the gate. Bernie's voice can be heard although the man himself is not seen:

BERNIE
(unseen; calling)
That you, Mr. Kenmore?

BRYAN (O.S.)
Yes, Bernie. Open up!

Bernie steps out from behind one of the stone posts; he carries a rifle at port arms.

BERNIE
Sure, Mr. Kenmore. Come on ahead.

199 ANOTHER ANGLE

Bryan drives the jeep up close to the barricade; Bernie doesn't make a move to get the car out of the way.

200 CLOSER ANGLE

> BRYAN
> Well - how about it?

> BERNIE
> (he grins; touches
> his cap)
> Right away...Just wanted to get
> a good look at you...

Absentmindedly he <u>scratches his chest</u>.

201 CLOSEUP - BRYAN

As he reacts to Bernie's unconscious - but meaningful - gesture.

> BERNIE (O.S.)
> Can't be too careful...

202 MED. TWO SHOT

Bernie turns to walk towards the blocking car; Bryan jumps out of the jeep - gun in hand.

> BRYAN
> Hold it. Bernie!

Bernie stops; he starts to turn.

> BRYAN
> Stand still! Throw down your rifle!

Bernie obeys.

> BRYAN
> Now - raise your hands! - And turn
> around - slowly!

Bernie does; Bryan cautiously walks up to him.

203 CLOSE TWO SHOT

Bernie, with his hands held high over his head, looks scared - yet defiant; Bryan is grim; he holds his gun unwaveringly pointed at Bernie; suddenly he rips open the man's shirt front; Bernie's chest is clean - free from any sign of rash!

(CONTINUED)

203 (CONTINUED)

>BRYAN
>(surprised)
>You're clean!..But - you scratched yourself!...

Bernie lets his hands sink down; gently he pushes Bryan's gun aside.

>BERNIE
>(with great relief)
>Great guns, Mr. Kenmore - but you scared me half to death! I sure thought I was a goner! I sure thought you'd gotten to be one of - them!

>BRYAN
>That's exactly what I thought about you!

>BERNIE
>(astonished)
>Me? Why?!

>BRYAN
>(sheepishly)
>You scratched your chest!

>BERNIE
>What? Oh! Yeah - guess I did at that! Most everybody does...One of them blasted, dive-bombing mosquitos must'a got me last night...

>BRYAN
>(he grins)
>Sorry, if I startled you.

>BERNIE
>That's okay. I'll do the same for you some day!

>BRYAN
>I hope not! Now - let's get that crate out of the way...I've got to see Professor Watkins right away!

>BERNIE
>(he touches his cap)
>Yes, Sir, Mr. Kenmore!

204   WIDER ANGLE

Bryan returns to his jeep; Bernie picks up his rifle and goes towards the car blocking the gateway...

                                        DISSOLVE:

205   INT. WATKINS' OFFICE - DAY - MED. CLOSEUP - ART - PULL BACK

Art looks angry; CAMERA PULLS BACK to a MED. GROUP SHOT including WATKINS, BRYAN, DIANE and TIM; there is an air of tension in the room.

                    ART
        ...you made a mess of it! I should
        have gone myself!..

                    BRYAN
        I tell you the Sheriff has changed...
        He's infected! He's got that rash!..

                    ART
        Why? Because he scratched his chest?

                    BRYAN
        Yes!

                    ART
        Does that mean he's infected? Does
        it? Can you be sure!

Bryan glances towards the window; he remembers Bernie.

                    BRYAN
                (hesitantly)
        No-o...

                    ART
                (still angry)
        All right -- so what do we do now
        that Bryan has alienated the Sheriff?

                    WATKINS
        This matter has grown too big for
        the local authorities already...

                    BRYAN
        There's no telling how fast the in-
        fection may spread...

                                        (CONTINUED)

205 (CONTINUED)

               DIANE
     They all seem to band together...
     Pretty soon they'll control every-
     thing!

               WATKINS
     Exactly! We don't know what this
     strange disease is - nor how it
     spreads...

               DIANE
     What can we do?

               WATKINS
     We must alert the government...I'll
     call the Governor!

He goes to the telephone; picks it up.

206 CLOSE SHOT - WATKINS

He frowns; he jiggles the phone.

               WATKINS
     The line is dead!

207 GROUP SHOT

Art hurries to Watkins' side; he takes the phone out of
his hand; he tries to make contact; then he throws the
receiver on the table in disgust.

               ART
     The wires! They've cut the telephone
     wires!

               WATKINS
          (stunned)
     They've isolated us!

Suddenly there is a distant shot from the outside -
another a little closer; Bryan springs into action.

               BRYAN
     Here they come!

He runs for the door, grabbing a rifle on the way; the
other men follow him during:

                              (CONTINUED)

207   (CONTINUED)

>   BRYAN
>   Grab the guns!..Diane - stay here!..
>   Come on!

They run out the door.

208   EXT. CAR BARRICADE AT GATEWAY - DAY - MED. WIDE SHOT

Bernie and Sammy are peering around the barricade down the road; Bryan and the others come running on to the scene taking cover behind the wall.

>   BRYAN
>   What's up, Bernie?

>   SAMMY
>   (excitedly)
>   Me! Me! They shoot me!..

>   BERNIE
>   Someone took a pot shot at Sammy,
>   here.

>   SAMMY
>   They shoot me, Professor! Shoot
>   me good! See!

He picks up an old strawhat; sticks his finger through a neat, round hole.

>   SAMMY
>   Ver-ry close sure enough!

>   BRYAN
>   What happened?

>   BERNIE
>   Sammy wanted to go down to the old
>   campus...no sooner did he stick his
>   head outside, some blame sniper took
>   a shot at him!

>   SAMMY
>   I shoot back all right...Don't hit
>   nothing.

>   BRYAN
>   Keep a close lookout, Bernie.

>   BERNIE
>   Yes, Sir...

Bryan turns to Watkins, Art and Tim.

209 FOUR SHOT

BRYAN
Looks like they're really determined to bottle us up in here...I suggest no one tries to leave the Science Building area just now...

TIM
Do you think they'll attack us in force?

BRYAN
Sooner or later - yes! My bluff with the Sheriff may keep them off for a while...

ART
We can't hold on here forever!

BRYAN
No - we can't. We'll have to establish contact with someone outside...

ART
Naturally - but how?

BRYAN
First things first. We must think about our safety...put some teeth in my bluff.

ART
What do you mean?

BRYAN
I deliberately gave the Sheriff the idea we'd rigged up some unpleasant surprise for any would-be intruders... We'll have to get it up!

ART
Talk sense!

BRYAN
We'll rig a dummy gimmick...something that looks dangerous...

TIM
Hey!..That's a great idea! It'll scare the pants off them!

(CONTINUED)

209   (CONTINUED)

                    BRYAN
          It'll make them think twice before
          they attack again...Give us some
          time...

                    ART
          All right - it might work...Then
          what?

                    BRYAN
          Then tonight, when it's dark, Tim
          and I'll make our way to town...

                    WATKINS
          Try to get to the hospital...Dr.
          Sokol...He may have found out some-
          thing about that confounded infec-
          tion...That's what's on the bottom
          of all this!

                    BRYAN
          Right!

210   ANOTHER ANGLE

       Bernie in the b.g. has been listening; he turns to the
       men.

                    BERNIE
               (he touches his cap)
          Begging your pardon, Mr. Kenmore...
          I'd like to volunteer to go with you
          ...I've been on plenty patrols in the
          Army...

                    BRYAN
          Thank you, Bernie...But we need some-
          one here - with military training...

                    BERNIE
          As you say, Sir...

                    BRYAN
          Okay...Let's get to work on that
          gimmick!..

                                        DISSOLVE:

211   EXT. WALL AND GATEWAY - NIGHT - PAN SHOT

The CAMERA PANS the top of the wall; at various intervals a collection of weird, complicated contraptions stud the wall and flank the gateway; made of twisted antennae, metal cones and coils and other devices, connected by wires and cords, their menacing shapes are silhouetted against the night sky; near the gateway a couple of floodlights illuminate the two most formidable looking gadgets. CAMERA PANS down to the base of the wall near the gateway to a MED. SHOT. Bryan, Tim, Art, Diane and Bernie are standing there; Sammy can be seen near the car barricade.

> BRYAN
> (in a low voice)
> I'm counting on you, Bernie.
>
> BERNIE
> Yes, Sir!
> (this time his touch-
> to-the cap is an actual
> salute)
> Good luck!
>
> BRYAN
> Thanks...

Bryan, Tim, Art and Diane start to walk quickly along the wall.

212   EXT. ANOTHER PART OF THE WALL - NIGHT - MED. SHOT - SMALL DOOR

Bryan, Tim, Art and Diane come up to the door. Slowly and cautiously Bryan slides aside a bolt and opens the door; he looks out, then turns to the others.

> BRYAN
> All clear!
>
> DIANE
> (she is looking
> at Bryan)
> Take care - both of you!
>
> TIM
> We'll be okay, Diane...
>
> DIANE
> It's a long way...The moon is so bright!

(CONTINUED)

212   (CONTINUED)

>   BRYAN
>   We'll make it...We'll be all right
>   once we're in town...

He looks out again.

>   BRYAN
>   Come on, Tim.

The two men quietly slip through the door; Art bolts it behind them; Diane looks at the closed door - then up to the top of the high wall...

213   TWO SHOT - DIANE AND ART

Art is scowling jealously.

>   ART
>   Aren't you getting a little too
>   concerned with that "boyscout",
>   Diane?

>   DIANE
>   Art!...

>   ART
>   (insinuating)
>   He might get the wrong idea!

>   DIANE
>   (cooly)
>   I don't think so!

>   ART
>   (getting angry)
>   Well I do! And I don't like it!

>   DIANE
>   I'm sorry, Art, but you'll have to
>   realize that my life is _still_ my own
>   affair!

>   ART
>   (sarcastically)
>   Is it?

>   DIANE
>   Yes -- it is!

>   ART
>   We'll see, Diane!

(CONTINUED)

74.

213   (CONTINUED)

He turns abruptly and walks off; Diane looks after him; then she again looks up to the top of the high wall.

214   CLOSEUP - DIANE

She looks worried and concerned...

DISSOLVE:

215   EXT. VILLAGE STREET - NIGHT - LONG SHOT

It is a bright, moonlit evening - but there are no lights in the houses. There is a strange, ominous feeling of imminent danger in the air (music will help set the mood); few people are abroad; those who can be seen walk purposefully and without any more than a cursory look at one another; gone is the friendly, neighborly atmosphere of the little town, which Bryan encountered before...

All of the townspeople on the street - men and women alike - have the front of their shirts and blouses ripped open, so the tell-tale streaky rash on their chests can be plainly seen.

216   ANOTHER ANGLE FEATURING GARAGE AND REPAIR SHOP

Off to one side of the area are stacked some old tires and other junk; there is a small movement behind the tire stacks.

217   CLOSE SHOT - AREA BEHIND TIRES

Bryan and Tim are crouched there, watching the people incredulously; they talk in whispers.

                    TIM
        What do you make of it, Bryan?

                    BRYAN
        They're all infected! Every one
        of them!..

                    TIM
        We'll have to wait till there's
        no one around...try and get to...

                    BRYAN
                (urgently)
        Quiet!..Look!..

218 LONG SHOT - STREET - BRYAN'S P.O.V.

   Down the street comes a group of people led by a boy of about ten years of age; they all display the rash on their chests; they look grim and dangerous and utterly ruthless; among them is Sergeant Strauss, the friendly, good-natured officer, who used to guard the campus...

   Another man passes them going in the other direction on the street; his shirt covers his chest; he is stopped roughly by the mob.

219 CLOSE GROUP SHOT

   Strauss faces the stranger grimly; without a word he takes hold of the man's shirt -

220 TWO SHOT

   Strauss savagely rips the stranger's shirt down the front; the streaky rash covers his chest; the man displays absolutely no reaction.

   > STRAUSS
   > (gruffly)
   > Keep it open!..So we know you!..

221 GROUP SHOT

   > BOY
   > (impatiently)
   > Come on, Mister!...It's right over there!..

   The stranger, without a word, continues on his way, and the mob again purposefully follows the boy.

222 CLOSE TWO SHOT - BRYAN AND TIM

   They look at each other grimly; then watch the mob.

223 MED. LONG SHOT - STREET

   The mob comes to a halt in front of a small house; they stand in a threatening, silent group; the house appears closed and quiet; the boy begins to call:

   > BOY
   > Mom! Hey, Mom!..Come on out!..
   > Mom!...

224   CLOSE SHOT - BOY

There is no response; the boy <u>scratches his chest</u>.

>   BOY
> Mom! Come on out, Mom...

225   WIDE SHOT - BRYAN'S P.O.V.

The house remains silent; with a sudden surge the mob all at once makes a rush for the closed door; almost immediately it gives way to their pressure - and part of the grim mob press inside...

Suddenly there is a piercing scream from inside the house - and almost at the same time the figure of a young girl (Nancy Hollis) comes dashing around from the back of the house; the scream from the house is repeated - ending abruptly, as the young girl runs in wild terror to the street - and on towards the garage...

She is discovered almost immediately; cries of "Get her!" - "Stop the girl!" - and "Don't let her get away!" arise from the mob left outside the house - as they at once sprint after the panic-stricken girl in pursuit.

226   CLOSE TWO SHOT - BRYAN AND TIM

Bryan makes a move as if to run to help the girl; Tim puts a huge hand on his shoulder, restraining him.

227   MED. LONG SHOT - STREET - BRYAN'S P.O.V.

The girl stumbles; she has almost reached the garage area; at once the mob is upon her; they haul her to her feet.

228   CLOSE GROUP SHOT

Two hard-faced women are holding the girl by her arms; she looks frantic with terror; Strauss comes through the mob to confront her.

229   CLOSER ANGLE

The girl looks at the officer; her eyes are wide with desperate fear.

>   NANCY
> Please!..Please, don't!..Please, don't!..

(CONTINUED)

77.

229   (CONTINUED)

Utterly disregarding her pleas Strauss reaches up - and tears open her blouse...Her chest is clean and smooth!.. A sigh goes through the mob...

Strauss takes out a pocket knife - and flicks it open.

>   NANCY
>   (frantic with horror)
>   No...NO...NO!..

230   CLOSE TWO SHOT - BRYAN AND TIM

They look horror-stricken.

231   CLOSE GROUP SHOT

Nancy is sobbing uncontrollably; Strauss is holding the knife in front of her; suddenly he brings it down sharply on his own thumb - opening a cut; almost in the same instant one of the women reaches out and rakes her sharp fingernails across the girl's shoulder - laying open a row of ugly gashes...

Nancy shrieks a terror-laden scream; Strauss draws his bleeding thumb over the open gashes on the girl's shoulder...

232   WIDER ANGLE

All of a sudden everyone in the mob seems to lose interest in the girl; the two women let go of her, and she sinks to the ground; and then - paying her not the slightest attention - the mob disperses...

233   TWO SHOT - BRYAN AND TIM

They look almost sick at what they have witnessed.

>   BRYAN
>   (shocked)
>   They infected her! They deliberately
>   infected her!
>   TIM
>   (he growls deep in
>   his throat)
>   Beasts!..Like - savage beasts!

(CONTINUED)

233   (CONTINUED)

>   BRYAN
>   (in a hurried whisper)
> Tim...That girl...She's only just
> been infected...We can't risk going
> to the hospital - not now...

>   TIM
> But we've got to find out about
> that infection...

>   BRYAN
> We'll have to do it ourselves!..

>   TIM
> What are you going to do?

>   BRYAN
> We'll take her back with us...Perhaps we can help her...at the same
> time we learn about the sickness...

>   TIM
> There's nobody around.

They both cautiously look out...

234   LONG SHOT - STREET - BRYAN'S P.O.V.

The street is empty except for Nancy, who lies on the ground a few yards in front of Bryan's and Tim's hiding place, miserably huddled in a lonely heap.

235   MED. SHOT - ACROSS BRYAN AND TIM TO NANCY IN THE STREET

>   BRYAN
> Let's go!

The two men quickly run from their hiding place; they reach the dazed girl; hurriedly they pick her up and dash back to the safety of their hiding place carrying her between them.

236   THREE SHOT

Bryan and Tim try to make the girl comfortable; she seems semi-delirious; she keeps muttering; only occasionally is she intelligible.

(CONTINUED)

236 (CONTINUED)

> NANCY
> ...let me...alone...

Bryan wipes her face.

> NANCY
> (as if in agony)
> ...get out...get out!..

> TIM
> What's she talking about?

> BRYAN
> She's delirious...

He watches her with concern.

> BRYAN (cont'd)
> I wish I could get her back right
> away...but we'll have to wait till
> it gets darker...

Nancy keeps murmuring disturbedly; CAMERA DOLLIES in towards her, during:

> TIM
> She's a sick kid, all right...

> BRYAN
> Poor girl...That was the <u>sure</u> way
> to get infected...

Camera is in a CLOSEUP of NANCY; she looks feverish; her face is moist with perspiration; her eyes are wild; her dry lips keep moving...

> DISSOLVE:

237 INT. SMALL STORE ROOM - NIGHT - CLOSE SHOT - DIANE

She looks concerned and compassionate; she is looking down; CAMERA PULLS BACK to a MED. WIDE SHOT.

The room is s small store room used for the storage of various scientific materials, chemicals, equipment and the like; there are several steel shelves pushed to one side and partly filled with bottles, cans, glass apparatus and boxes. Diane is standing at the head of a cot placed in the center of the room; on the cot lies Nancy; her head rests on a pillow, and she is covered

(CONTINUED)

237 (CONTINUED)

with a blanket; her arms lie on top of the blanket; a sheet has been torn in strips and one of these strips has been securely tied around each of the girl's wrists and then down around the cot holding her in place; Nancy's eyes are wide open and alert; gone is the feverish, delirious look - although little beads of sweat still pearl her forehead - but, if anything, she now looks dangerous!

In the b.g. Fanny, the Cleaning Woman, a woman around sixty, is wetting a cloth in a basin of cold water; periodically she wipes Nancy's brow.

Bryan is at the side of the cot; he pulls the cover down enough to see the girl's chest; the streaky, red rash is clearly evident.

          BRYAN
    The rash has already developed...
    doesn't take long...

He picks up a syringe and takes a sample of Nancy's blood, during:

          DIANE
    Must we keep her tied like that?

          BRYAN
    She'll be comfortable enough...She
    isn't herself, yet...She's dangerous...
    If she can infect you, she will!
        (he looks up at Diane
        with concern)
    I wish you wouldn't stay here!..

          DIANE
    I want to...

          BRYAN
    Maybe Tim...

          DIANE
        (firmly)
    No, Bryan! Dad and Sammy are re-
    lieving Bernie on the gate. Every-
    one has a job to do. This one's
    mine - and Fanny's!

          FANNY
    We'll take good care of little Nancy,
    here. Never you fear, Mr. Kenmore...

(CONTINUED)

237   (CONTINUED - 2)

                    BRYAN
          Nancy?

                    DIANE
          That's her name. Nancy Hollis.
          Fanny knows her family. Says
          she's a very nice girl...

Bryan is finished; he stands up.

                    BRYAN
          All the same...I don't want you
          alone with her...

238   TWO SHOT

Diane gives Bryan a warm smile.

                    DIANE
          I won't, Bryan. Fanny'll be with
          me.

                    BRYAN
          I worry about you...

She puts her hand on Bryan's arm; it is almost a caress.

                    DIANE
          You don't have to...

                    BRYAN
          Be careful!

                    DIANE
          I will.

                                        DISSOLVE:

239   INT. B LABORATORY - DAY - CLOSE SHOT - OBJECT

Several thin wires run into the front opening on the object; CAMERA PULLS BACK to a MED. SHOT; in the b.g. the door can be seen: in the f.g. Watkins and Art are engrossed in their work with the object; the wires from the opening connect with a series of complicated looking electro-magnetic equipment, meters and guages; Watkins is manipulating the equipment; Art is observing and recording the readings on a meter dial.

                                        (CONTINUED)

239 (CONTINUED)

      ART
     (reading)
  Reading twenty...Reading twenty...

Suddenly the door in the b.g. bursts open and Bryan comes running in holding a couple of microscope slides in his hand; he runs to the two men.

      BRYAN
     (excited)
  Professor Watkins!..

      ART
  ...Reading forty...

      WATKINS
  Quiet Bryan!

      ART
  ...Reading fifty...

      BRYAN
  But Professor...This is very imp...

      WATKINS
     (sharply)
  Be quiet!

      ART
  ...Reading sixty...

      WATKINS
  Stand by!

He flips a switch.

240 INSERT - CLOSEUP METER DIAL

The dial is graded from zero in the center to plus and minus one hundred; the needle is at <u>plus sixty</u>...Suddenly it literally jumps to <u>minus sixty</u>.

      ART (O.S.)
  Complete reversal!

241 MED. SHOT - OVERLAPPING

      ART
  Reading minus sixty!

          (CONTINUED)

241 (CONTINUED)

      WATKINS
     (with satisfaction)
As I thought...Reversal of the
magnetic field...
     (he glares at Bryan)
How many times have I asked you not
to come barging in like that in the
middle of an experiment...?

      BRYAN
I've found the cause of the sickness!!

      WATKINS
...The first thing a scientist should...
     (he suddenly realizes
     what Bryan said)
You _what_!?

      ART
What is it?!

      BRYAN
The dust! The dust particles from
space! Only they aren't dust - they
are spores..._living spores_ - in dormant stage!

      WATKINS
     (startled)
Living Spores?

      BRYAN
Yes! only - they're different from
any I've ever seen..._spore-like dormant micro-cells_!

      WATKINS
Are you sure?

      BRYAN
     (eagerly)
Of course, I'm sure!

He gives the slides he is holding to Watkins, who proceeds to examine them under a microscope, during:

      BRYAN
Here - look!

      ART
     (skeptically)
How did you find out?

         (CONTINUED)

241   (CONTINUED - 2)

> BRYAN
> I was examining a blood sample I'd taken from Nancy - the infected girl we brought back... I noticed a few dark specks among the leucocytes... I prepared slides of them - and on a hunch compared them with the slides of the space dust... They were the same!

> WATKINS
> (looking up from the microscope)
> They are the same! But what makes you so certain they're alive?

Bryan quickly changes the slides in the microscope.

> BRYAN
> This!

Watkins leans to examine it.

> BRYAN
> It is one of the particles from the dust we retained... I watched it come alive and grow with incredible speed - when I placed it in a drop of my own blood!

> WATKINS
> Amazing!

> BRYAN
> Professor. You see what this means... The sickness is an infection from space - an Alien Plague!

> WATKINS
> (with growing realization)
> ...Let loose when the spores were scattered to the wind!..

> ART
> ...constantly multiplying - and infecting everyone!..

> BRYAN
> Exactly...

(CONTINUED)

241 (CONTINUED - 3)

>
> WATKINS
> But it doesn't answer one vital question Bryan...Why do these infected people attack _us_?

Bryan looks seriously at Watkins.

>
> BRYAN
> I have a theory about that, Professor...It may hold the answer...
>
> WATKINS
> Let us hear it...
>
> BRYAN
> The plague is caued by micro-organism ...a symbiotic, microscopic cell incapable of active life - or reproduction - away from the living cells of its host..._Like_ the influenza virus ...or the _polio_ virus, for example...
>
> WATKINS
> Go on...
>
> BRYAN
> Like our sporozoa - or sporogenetic plants - this micro-cell from space can form what amounts to _spores_ - in that way entering a state of suspended animation...Only when it again enters into a symbiotic relationship with a host, does it come to life...
>
> ART
> We know this, Bryan...
>
> WATKINS
> Let him finish...
> (to Bryan)
> Come to the point...
>
> BRYAN
> I think that when the _alien_ micro-cell enters a host - in _this_ case a human being - it _takes over_ the _will_ and control of _this_ host..._with a will and intelligence of its own!_
>
> ART
> Preposterous!..

(CONTINUED)

241 (CONTINUED - 4)

                BRYAN
Why? Art? Why? Because its alien to earth?!

                ART
An intelligent germ!..Really!!

                BRYAN
Why not? How else can you explain the actions of the infected people? Life as we know it began with one-celled creatures...

                WATKINS
And you think that - somewhere - there exists one-celled life whose function is intelligence!
        (he looks thoughtful)
Astounding...But - it is possible!

                ART
And what is your explanations for the attack on us?

                BRYAN
Perhaps an attempt to regain control of - that!

He points to the space object; the two scientists are startled as they realize the logical reasoning behind Bryan's statement.

                WATKINS
If you are right, Bryan...What then?

                BRYAN
If there is intelligence - there must be an area of communication...We must find it!

                ART
What about that girl - Nancy?...

                BRYAN
No use...She's fallen into a state of sullen apathy...

                WATKINS
Then - how do you propose to communicate with - with a germ?!

                        (CONTINUED)

241   (CONTINUED - 5)

        BRYAN
  There is a way...But I'll need a
  lot of help...

        WATKINS
  You'll have it!..

           DISSOLVE:

242   INT. SMALL EXPERIMENTAL LABORATORY ROOM - MED. SHOT

Bryan is sitting at a microscope; the room is lit with a single lamp shining on the microscope; Bryan is engrossed in his work; Diane enters.

        DIANE
  Bryan!..

        BRYAN
    (without looking up)
  Yes, Diane?

        DIANE
  Sorry to disturb you - but Professor Watkins wants your tables
  for the tissue culture...

        BRYAN
  On the table - over there...

Diane goes to a table - tries to find the papers in the gloom; during:

        BRYAN
  Is he ready to start it?

        DIANE
  Right away...

        BRYAN
  Well - if I can't lick this problem
  here - the whole thing may be no
  good...

        DIANE
  What's holding you up?

        BRYAN
  I'm trying to make an agent that
  will stain the micro-cells once
  they grow out of the spore stage...

           (CONTINUED)

242 (CONTINUED)

> DIANE
> Stain them?

> BRYAN
> Color them - so they can be seen...
> Otherwise they're invisible...

> DIANE
> Oh...

She rummages for the papers...

> BRYAN
> If you can't see, put on the light
> for a minute...

> DIANE
> All right...

She walks to the wall and flips a switch; instead of the overhead light going on a large, intricate looking lamp standing on the floor begins to glow with an eerie light; Diane sees his mistake...

> DIANE
> Oops!..

She flips off the big lamp and turns on the overhead light: Bryan whirls upon her.

> BRYAN
> Diane! What did you do?!

> DIANE
> (startled)
> Do? Why - nothing! I just put on
> that lamp by mistake!..

> BRYAN
> The ultra-violet lamp!..For a moment
> I saw something!..Turn it on again!..

Diane obeys; he turns off the overhead light and flips on the ultra-violet lamp; Bryan bends over his microscope...

> BRYAN
> There it is! Faint- but I can see
> it! The light is staining it!...

(CONTINUED)

242   (CONTINUED - 2)

>   DIANE
>   Is that good?...
>
>   BRYAN
>   Good?! That's what I've been
>   looking for!

He gets up; turns off the ultra-violet lamp and flips on the overhead light; he goes over to Diane at the table, during:

>   BRYAN
>   A _light bath_! Ultra-violet - infra-
>   red - maybe a combination...And we
>   can see every micro-cell - even if
>   they enter the air, we might see them
>   as a mist...

Diane has found the papers he came for; Bryan turns to her.

>   BRYAN
>   Tell Watkins - I'll be ready when
>   he is - _thanks to you_!..

                                        DISSOLVE:

243   INT. EXPERIMENTAL LAB - CLOSE SHOT - LARGE GLASS BOWL

The bowl is quite big; it is filled with a special tissue culture, a large, nearly transparent, gelatinous mass that quivers at the slightest touch; a thermometer is permanently dipped into the jelly-like substance, and a couple of glass nozzles on long rubber tubes, hooked up to a couple of bottles, hanging from stands, are inserted into the culture.

The CAMERA PULLS BACK to a MED. SHOT. Bryan and Diane are present in the little laboratory. It is a specially rigged room; along one wall is a large, thick-paned observation window; the room itself holds a metal table on which stands the culture bowl; there is a tape recorder set-up complete with microphone; and ringing the room are several inter-connected stands of light appratus.

Bryan is checking the culture thermometer; Diane is unpacking a surgical mask and laying it out on the table.

                                        (CONTINUED)

243   (CONTINUED)

> BRYAN
> There...The tissue culture is doing just great...

> DIANE
> (concerned)
> I wish you wouldn't go through with this, Bryan...

> BRYAN
> Now, don't you worry...Everything will work out...

> DIANE
> But - suppose something does go wrong?...You might be infected!

Bryan goes over to the tape recorder; he checks to see that it is in working order.

> BRYAN
> Nothing can happen as long as we only let the spores develop in the culture...

He lets the recorder spin for a couple of seconds; then he shuts it off.

> DIANE
> What if it doesn't work?

Bryan turns to look at the serious girl.

244   CLOSE TWO SHOT

> BRYAN
> Then there's only one alternative... I'll have to infect myself...

> DIANE
> No!

> BRYAN
> It would be the only way left to communicate with the alien life form...

> DIANE
> No, Bryan! Not you!..Maybe - someone else...

(CONTINUED)

244   (CONTINUED)

                    BRYAN
                  (seriously)
          Who, Diane?...

245   ANOTHER ANGLE - WIDER SHOT

      Tim is standing just inside the door to the corridor.

                    TIM
          Me!

      Diane and Bryan turn towards Tim - startled; Tim walks
      over to them; CAMERA DOLLIES in to a CLOSE THREE SHOT,
      during:

                    BRYAN & DIANE
          Tim!
          Dad!

                    TIM
          I should be the one! It was all my
          fault in the first place...

      He obviously feels very guilty and bitter.

                    BRYAN
          Nonsense...It was an accident...

                    TIM
          That I was responsible for! It's up
          to me...I'm just as healthy as you
          are.

                    BRYAN
          It isn't a matter of health, Tim...

                    TIM
          What then?

                    BRYAN
                  (slowly)
          You'd be entering into a symbiotic
          relationship with this alien life
          form...

                    TIM
                  (defiantly)
          Okay!..

                                              (CONTINUED)

245   (CONTINUED - 2)

>   BRYAN
> ...You'd have to do so with an open mind...You'd have to analyze and report everything that happens to you - as the organism gradually takes over ...and then try to communicate with it...

Diane is watching the two men anxiously; her eyes look haunted...

>   TIM
> All right! I'm willing!!..

>   BRYAN
> I know...But - Tim...

Tim goes to Bryan.

246   CLOSE TWO SHOT

>   TIM
>   (earnestly)
> Don't you see, Bryan...I blame myself - for everything that's happened...

>   BRYAN
>   (remonstrating)
> Tim...

>   TIM
>   (stopping him)
> No...I have to live with myself... You _must_ give me this chance...

>   BRYAN
> I - can't...

247   WIDER ANGLE

Diane goes up to her father.

>   DIANE
> Oh, Dad...Don't you see what Bryan's trying to tell you...

>   TIM
>   (bewildered)
> No. What?

(CONTINUED)

247   (CONTINUED)

>   DIANE
> Dad...You'd have to have a trained
> mind to cope with a thing like that!
> A <u>scientist's</u> mind!...

Tim suddenly realizes; he looks abashed...

>   TIM
> Yes...I see...I only wanted to
> help...

>   BRYAN
> I know. Thanks, Tim...

248   WIDER ANGLE

Art comes in through the door; he carries several light tubes and bulbs.

>   ART
> Hey...Give me a hand with these!

Tim and Bryan go to help him; they begin to install the tubes and bulbs in the light apparatus standing around the room.

249   TWO SHOT - DIANE AND ART

They are placing a long tube in its sockets.

>   ART
>   (sarcastically)
> Our boy genius really had himself
> a brainstorm this time!

>   DIANE
>   (defensively)
> I'm sure it'll work.

>   ART
> Staining the micro-cells with a bath
> of different light rays? Ridiculous!

250   WIDER ANGLE

Watkins enters; he is gingerly carrying the little glass beaker with the remaining spores; he carefully places it on the table.

(CONTINUED)

250 (CONTINUED)

> WATKINS
> Here are the spores from the safe...
> Are you about ready, Bryan?

> BRYAN
> Just about...

> WATKINS
> Fine...We'll watch from the corridor...Come on...

He starts for the door; the others follow.

251 TWO SHOT - BRYAN AND DIANE

She puts her hand on Bryan's arm.

> DIANE
> (softly)
> Please...be careful!..

> BRYAN
> (he smiles a little
> smile; then he touches
> her hand)
> I will...

252 ANOTHER ANGLE

Everybody leaves the room; as Art is about to close the door, Bryan calls:

> BRYAN
> Remember, Art. Keep the door closed till I say it's safe...No matter what happens!

> ART
> All right.

He closes the door; through the window the four onlookers can be seen in the corridor - watching tensely; Diane goes up to her father; she takes his arm - looks up at him - worriedly; Tim gives her a reassuring nod.

253 CLOSE SHOT - ART

He frowns at this by-play.

254 LAB

Bryan is putting on the surgical mask; he then reaches for a pair of dark goggles and puts them on too; then he starts the tape-recorder.

> BRYAN
> (his voice is being
> picked up by the mike)
> Stand by...Put your goggles on, please...

255 CORRIDOR

Watkins, Art, Tim and Diane all put goggles over their eyes; through the window into the little lab Bryan can be seen.

> BRYAN (cont'd)
> Light bath going on...

He flips a few switches; the various lights go on - bathing the entire lab in an eerie glow.

Bryan walks to the table; carefully he picks up the beaker with the spores...

> BRYAN
> Here goes!

Quickly he empties the spores into the tissue culture.

256 REACTION SHOTS

As Watkins, Art, Tim and Diane strain to see what is happening...

257 CLOSE SHOT - BRYAN

He is bent over the culture; suddenly he draws back...

258 CLOSE SHOT - THE CULTURE

It is seething and boiling; in front of our very eyes it grows into a pulsating, slimy mass - growing and growing...

259   ANOTHER ANGLE TAKING IN BRYAN

The tissue mass is sending up a thick 'appendage'...
Suddenly it seems to 'turn its attention' towards Bryan,
who is watching with fascination next to it...

260   WIDER ANGLE - BRYAN AND CULTURE IN F.G. - WINDOW TO
CORRIDOR IN B.G.

Outside Watkins, Art, Tim and Diane are watching intently
...All at once the substance in the culture bowl begins
to grow with alarming speed; before Bryan - or the incredulous spectators standing aghast in the corridor outside - can realize what is happening, the translucent,
light-stained form of a man quickly grows from the culture...And as Bryan shrinks back - this alien form
swiftly and determinedly advances upon him...

261   CORRIDOR - WINDOW TO LAB

With a growl deep in his throat Tim leaps across the
corridor; with one blow of his fist he smashes the
glass in a case on the wall holding a fireaxe; in one
moment he grabs the axe and hurls himself at the lab
door...

262   LAB

The door bursts open - and Tim - his axe held high -
comes rushing into the room, intent upon destroying the
alien creature by force...Suddenly Bryan rips off his
face mask and shouts with unexpected force:

>   BRYAN
> Stop!

Stunned by the force and vehemence of Bryan's command
Tim stops dead in his tracks.

>   BRYAN (cont'd)
> Leave us alone!

As the dazed Tim slowly backs off, the ghostly, tenuous
alien man-form - grimly advances upon Bryan...

And while the others watch in horror and uncomprehending
shock - the Alien Micro Man reaches Bryan - and slowly
seems to ooze into him, merging with him!..

(CONTINUED)

262 (CONTINUED)

Immediately Bryan reels - then he catches himself - and mechanically he strides from the chamber to join the others in the corridor...And speaking in a strangely flat, monotonous voice he says:

     BRYAN
 We must - work -- together!..

Then, without warning - he collapses on the floor...

       DISSOLVE:

263 INT. WATKINS' OFFICE - DAY - CLOSE SHOT - BRYAN

He is sprawled in a large chair; his head is resting on the back; his eyes are closed; he is still unconscious...

CAMERA PULLS BACK to reveal Diane, Tim, Watkins and Art cautiously grouped around Bryan at a little distance...

Suddenly Bryan opens his eyes wide; he sits up...Diane starts towards him; Art holds her back...

     ART
 Wait!..

     DIANE
 Bryan!..Bryan! Are you all right?!

     BRYAN
   (slowly)
 Yes...I'm - all right...

     TIM
 The Alien!..We - saw him! He - He...

     BRYAN
 I know...

     WATKINS
 What do you feel, Bryan? Is - is he - taking over?...

     BRYAN
 No-o...

     ART
 So much for your intelligent micro-organism!

       (CONTINUED)

263 (CONTINUED)

              BRYAN
You're wrong, Art...He's there...

              TIM
Are you sure, Bryan? Maybe you aren't infected at all. If you <u>were</u>, you'd be out of your head by n<u>ow</u> - like Nancy...

              BRYAN
She was delirious only because her body was fighting the alien control ...There is no struggle for possession of my mind...

              ART
How do we know you aren't controlled right now?

              BRYAN
You don't!

Everyone looks startled - and a little apprehensive.

              ART
We know you're infected - and you talked very strangely before...

              BRYAN
That was - <u>he</u>...

              DIANE
He said for us to - work together... What did he mean?

              WATKINS
Can you communicate with him now, Bryan?

              BRYAN
             (resolutely)
I can do just one thing...I can willingly yield control of my mind - to him!..

Diane gives a little gasp; Bryan looks at her and smiles uncertainly; then he lowers his head as if concentrating ...The others watch him tensely...

264 ANOTHER ANGLE

Bryan looks up; his eyes look intently alert; there is about him a maturity and authority way beyond his own character; he is a person of great strength and self-assurance...His phraseology is distinctly different from that of Bryan...

                "BRYAN"
            (his voice seems firmer)
Do not be alarmed! Bryan - my host - will not be harmed...and neither will you...

                WATKINS
Who - _what_ - are you???

                "BRYAN"
I come from a solar system many light years from yours...I am of a race of beings, which only lives through the life of another...A race of one-celled micro-organisms - evolved from what you call the symbiotics - just like _man_ evolved from the anthropoids... I am _Norot_...

                WATKINS
A single cell!..

                TIM
But...I _saw_ you...The shape of a _man_!

                NOROT
Because the host I was about to enter, was a man...You would have seen me in the shape of any host I would enter...a dog...a bird...

                WATKINS
What do you want here? Why are all your...eh...companions - taking over our people? Creating conflict and violence?

Bryan/Norot looks at Watkins gravely; he seems deeply concerned.

                NOROT
There are only _two_ of us here...If others have been taken for hosts - it is by _Grag_ - and his seed...

                (CONTINUED)

264   (CONTINUED)

                    WATKINS
          I don't understand...

                    NOROT
          Each one of us can adopt a dormant
          life form...

                    WATKINS
          Like our spores?

                    NOROT
          Yes. When these spores enter a
          host they live - and can take
          over...

                    WATKINS
          Then each spore must actually in-
          herit the knowledge and memories
          of its ancestor!

                    NOROT
          They do. That is why we are near
          immortal...Grag - my companion -
          wants an army of his breed...

                    DIANE
          If it's true that you wish us no
          harm...Why should the other one -
          Grag - attack us - and try to kill
          us?

                    NOROT
          Not you!..He wants to destroy me!..

265   INT. SHERIFF MORGAN'S OFFICE - DAY - CLOSE SHOT -
      MORGAN/GRAG

      He is standing near the wall map of the community area.

                    MORGAN
                (ruthlessly)
          He must be destroyed! As long as
          Norot's spores are in existence we
          are not safe!

      CAMERA DOLLIES out to a WIDE SHOT. Gathered around Mor-
      gan are Sergeant Strauss, Officer Lawson, the Boy, the
      Careless Pedestrian, the man whose shirt was ripped open,
      the two women who held Nancy; all of them have open
      shirts and blouses so the tell-tale rash can be seen;
      they all look hard and determined.

                                              (CONTINUED)

265   (CONTINUED)

> MORGAN (cont'd)
> As far as we know he has not yet been able to enter a host...He has not yet had a chance to multiply, as we have...We must get to the ship and destroy him before he does!
>
> STRAUSS
> What about those defenses the men have rigged up out there?
>
> MORGAN
> We'll deal with them in due time...
>
> LAWSON
> May cost a lot of lives...
>
> MORGAN
> They're only hosts...We mustn't overplay our hand...time is on our side...In a few days we'll control every human being in this community...Then we can afford a mass attack.

CAMERA DOLLIES in to a C.U. of MORGAN, during:

> MORGAN
> We have found a world here with perhaps billions of hosts for the taking! They can offer very little resistance - except for Norot!

DISSOLVE:

266   INT. WATKINS' OFFICE - DAY - CLOSEUP - NOROT/BRYAN

He has the tense, authoritative expression which identifies control by the micro man; CAMERA PULLS BACK to include Watkins, Tim, Art and Diane, during:

> NOROT
> (speaking through Bryan)
> ...Our scout ship was sent out to locate other solar systems with life-bearing planets, for future expansion...
>
> DIANE
> And you found our solar system - and us...

(CONTINUED)

266 (CONTINUED)

> NOROT
> Yes...

> WATKINS
> (appalled)
> Your race wants to use mankind as hosts...taken by force!?

> NOROT
> (earnestly)
> Man is in danger! Let me tell you of my race...

CAMERA INTERCUTS reaction shots of Watkins, Art and Diane as they listen - spellbound - to Norot's story, told through Bryan...

> NOROT
> We have not been handicapped, as you have, with the complications of multiple cell structure and disease...We have long ago risen above the need for - a heart - lungs - a body with its many intricate organs...Our development has been towards mental power...Concentrated in a one cell organism.

> WATKINS
> (incensed)
> Whose purpose is to invade the minds of other beings!

> NOROT
> We still have a long way to go...We have not yet conquered ourselves spiritually...In Grag and his kind rules the desire for power and force...and they at the moment control our worlds...

> DIANE
> What about you?

> NOROT
> There are, among us, a few who revolt against the enslavement of hosts by superior mental force...I am one of these...We believe that we and our hosts must live to mutual benefit in a relationship desired by both...
> (continued)

(CONTINUED)

266 (CONTINUED - 2)

>   NOROT (cont'd)
>   A symbiosis of thought and intelli-
>   gence striving towards universal
>   wisdom, love and peace...A whole
>   greater than the sun of its parts.
>
>   ART
>   (bitterly)
>   Is that why you're here?
>
>   NOROT
>   When our space craft located your
>   solar system - and found it in-
>   habited - I caused a power failure
>   in the ship, hoping to fall into
>   your sun...Instead we crashed on
>   this planet...We were engulfed in
>   a viscous mass...our hosts perished
>   ...We entered into our 'spore stage"
>   and were held prisoners until now...
>
>   WATKINS
>   50,000 years!..
>
>   NOROT
>   In our "spore stage" - time has no
>   real meaning...50,000 years are like
>   5 minutes...
>
>   ART
>   But what about the expansion plans
>   of your race?
>
>   NOROT
>   They must be underway - even now!
>   My race will find your planet - even
>   if we find a way to stop Grag!...

Bryan suddenly relaxes; the tenseness leaves him - and he becomes his usual self...

>   DIANE
>   Bryan?...
>
>   BRYAN
>   Yes...
>
>   WATKINS
>   Bryan. The alien said...

(CONTINUED)

266 (CONTINUED - 3)

> BRYAN
> (interrupting)
> I know, Professor...Although only one of us at a time can control my brian - my speech...we both are aware of each other's intelligence...

> DIANE
> It's - frightening!...

> BRYAN
> No, Diane...I know Norot, now... I trust him!

> WATKINS
> Do you realize our situation? We're isolated here - completely isolated - just a handful of us - with knowledge of the greatest danger ever to confront mankind!

> BRYAN
> It's up to us to find a way to destroy the alien micro men outside...in the time we have left.

> ART
> Is Norot on the level - wanting to help us destroy them? His own race?

> BRYAN
> You heard what he said...He is like an underground fighter in Hitler's Nazi Germany...He will help!

> ART
> Then why not let him infect a lot of other people with his spores? Let them fight it out?

> BRYAN
> And turn the human race into a deadly battle field? No - Art!..

> TIM
> How could you know who'd win?

> BRYAN
> We must find a way to destroy the micro men without harming the human hosts...They are innocent victims...
> (continued)

(CONTINUED)

266   (CONTINUED - 4)

>   BRYAN (cont'd)
>   They, themselves, have no evil in-
>   tent...You don't punish a man be-
>   cause he gets infected with tuber-
>   culosis!..You simply try to kill
>   the TB germs...
>
>   DIANE
>   What about the antibiotics? Peni-
>   cillin? Terramycin?...What about
>   that strengthening agent you're
>   working on, Bryan?
>
>   BRYAN
>   The potentiator? It's still in the
>   research stage...
>
>   ART
>   Antibiotics are quite ineffective
>   against organisms like viruses...
>   And apparently the micro-men are
>   very similar to the viruses...
>
>   WATKINS
>   We must try them nevertheless! The
>   alien in that girl - Nancy - will
>   be our guinea pig. We'll start at
>   once...Come on, Bryan!!

He marches purposefully towards the door; Bryan and the others follow him, as he leaves; at the door Art de-tains Diane.

267   TWO SHOT

>   ART
>   Dee!...
>
>   DIANE
>   Yes, Art?
>
>   ART
>   (frowning)
>   I want you to be careful -
>
>   DIANE
>   Careful?...
>
>   ART
>   Of Bryan...

(CONTINUED)

267 (CONTINUED)

>
> DIANE
> Bryan!
>
> ART
> He's infected!
>
> DIANE
> He believes in Norot...So do I!
>
> ART
> His beliefs mean very little – under the circumstances!
>
> DIANE
> I'll make up my own mind, Art!...
>
> ART
> You'd be much wiser to do what I tell you...
>
> DIANE
> (cooly)
> You don't own me, Art!
>
> ART
> Stay away from him!..I warn you.

Diane looks angrily at Art; then she turns on her heel and leaves.

DISSOLVE:

268 INT. B LABORATORY - NIGHT - CLOSE SHOT - TEST TUBE

The test tube is filled with a dark liquid; it is sealed with a rubber cover over the opening; a hand is holding it; the other hand comes into the picture holding a syringe filled with a clear liquid; the needle on the syringe is stuck through the rubber cover and some of the clear liquid is injected into the test tube; the syringe is withdrawn, and the test tube is shaken gently; suddenly the dark liquid changes color to a completely clear liquid; CAMERA PULLS BACK to a MED. SHOT.

Bryan is alone in the laboratory; he replaces the test tube in a rack.

> BRYAN
> (tiredly)
> Number 179 - negative!..It's no good, Norot...

(CONTINUED)

268   (CONTINUED)

He seemingly answers himself - but with a different, more mechanical voice - the voice of Norot...

>   NOROT
>   Antibiotics do not hold the answer...

Bryan reaches for another test tube...

>   BRYAN
>   We have one more preparation left
>   ...might as well try it...

269   ANOTHER ANGLE

In the open door in the b.g. stands Diane; she is watching Bryan; she looks concerned.

>   NOROT
>   We must think of - another way...

Bryan passes a hand over his eyes; he is exhausted.

>   BRYAN
>   Our time may be running out...

Diane gets a resolute expression on her face; with deliberate cheer she calls to Bryan:

>   DIANE
>   Hey! Is that a private conversation?
>   Or can anyone join?

She walks over to Bryan.

>   DIANE
>   What are you doing? Practising to
>   be a ventriloquist?

Bryan laughs a little.

During the following he repeats the test tube experiment with the same result as before; discouragedly he places it in the rack.

>   BRYAN
>   You can keep me company for a while...

>   DIANE
>   Why don't you take a rest? Clear
>   your mind...You've been at it all
>   day...

(CONTINUED)

269   (CONTINUED)

>   BRYAN
>   We've got to find an answer - or
>   the whole human race may be doomed...
>
>   DIANE
>   (firmly)
>   But you won't!..If you exhaust your-
>   self - and Norot!

Bryan looks up at her quickly - but says nothing.

>   DIANE
>   (timidly)
>   Bryan...What's it like - to...to
>   have him with you?...

Bryan smiles.

>   BRYAN
>   I'm hardly aware of it - only when
>   we - talk...
>
>   DIANE
>   Does he - know...everything - about
>   you?

Bryan nods.

>   BRYAN
>   And he's made me the healthiest man
>   alive! There isn't an undesirable
>   germ or virus in my entire body! He
>   got rid of them all!..Like other
>   micro-organisms he has the power to
>   destroy germs...and look!..

He gets up; Diane follows him to a table; he takes a small, sharp knife or scalpel.

>   BRYAN
>   Watch!

He bares his arm.

270   CLOSE SHOT - BRYAN'S ARM

Bryan places the knife on his skin; quickly he makes a small incision; the blood at once flows out; Diane gives a small, involuntary outcry o.s.

271 CLOSE TWO SHOT

  Bryan holds up his arm with the bleeding wound; Diane watches, wide-eyed; Bryan picks up a piece of cloth.

      BRYAN
    This - too - is Norot's doing!

Quickly he rubs the cloth over the wound - cleaning it; the blood is gone - and the wound is closed and healed, as if it had never been there!

      DIANE
     (with a gasp)
    It's gone!

      BRYAN
    Norot can control my tissues -
    almost perfectly!

He shows her the unscarred arm.

      BRYAN (cont'd)
    I discovered it when I cut myself
    on a broken test tube...There are
    quite a few benefits to this symbiotic
    business!...

      DIANE
    With Norot - yes...But what about
    all those who have been taken over
    by - Grag? Will they be harmed -
    just as you are helped?

      BRYAN
    They won't be harmed - bodily...It's
    to the micro-men's own advantage to
    keep their hosts as healthy and strong
    as possible...

Diane puts her hand in wonder on Bryan's arm; slowly she starts to stroke the spot where the wound was a few seconds ago; then she looks up into Bryan's face; they stand very close together...Suddenly Bryan takes her in his arms and kisses her; she obviously belongs there!..

CAMERA SWISH PANS to the open door and ZOOMS in on a man standing there; it is Art; he scowls; he makes a movement as if to interfere; then he gets a thoughtful expression on his face - and quietly leaves.

272 TWO SHOT - BRYAN AND DIANE

They draw apart reluctantly; Diane looks radiant; she holds Bryan at arm's length.

>   DIANE
> What we need is a bit of fresh
> air!

                                        DISSOLVE:

273 EXT. LAWN IN FRONT OF ENTRANCE TO SCIENCE BUILDING - NIGHT - MED. LONG SHOT

Bryan and Diane come slowly walking, close together, down the path; they cut in over the lawn to a large tree, and sit down at its roots.

274 TWO SHOT - BRYAN AND DIANE

They look happy - and in love; Bryan takes Diane in his arms; they kiss - their embrace becomes more and more ardent; finally Diane gently but firmly breaks away...

>   DIANE
>   (softly)
> No, Bryan...no...

Bryan lets her go.

>   DIANE
> It's - it's been such a short time...

>   BRYAN
> I love you, Diane...

>   DIANE
> And I love you - very much...But
> we can't...

>   BRYAN
> Diane...

>   DIANE
> Yes?...

>   BRYAN
> Do you know how I feel about you -
> and us?...

>   DIANE
> I think I do.

                                        (CONTINUED)

274   (CONTINUED)

>   BRYAN
>   I read a poem once - years ago -
>   "The White Cliffs", it was called,
>   written during World War II. I
>   believe it went like this - at
>   least the passages that impressed
>   me so - would you like to hear it?
>
>   DIANE
>   Of course.
>
>   BRYAN
>   (he quotes softly)
>   "Lovers in peacetime
>   With fifty years to live,
>   Have time to tease and quarrel
>   And question what to give.
>   But lovers in wartime
>   Better understand
>   The fullness of living,
>   With death close at hand."
>
>   DIANE
>   It's beautiful...and true...Bryan -

She goes to him. They kiss tenderly...

>   BRYAN
>   Yes - ?
>
>   DIANE
>   I do love you...and - I guess - in
>   a way - we <u>are</u> at war!
>
>   BRYAN
>   Diane...If we get out of this...
>   will you marry me?
>
>   DIANE
>   No, dear! Not <u>if</u> - when! When
>   this is all over - I'll marry you!
>
>   BRYAN
>   I wish - I wish I could have your
>   confidence...

For a moment Bryan looks at her...Then he takes her in his arms; they kiss with mounting ardor; then they slowly sink down out of frame, as CAMERA PANS up to the sky seen through the branches of the trees...

A large dark cloud swirls across the night sky...

111.

275   EXT. - NIGHT - FULL SHOT OF WINDOW IN SCIENCE BUILDING

There is no light inside; the window is lit by the moonlight; slowly a shadow falls across it; CAMERA DOLLIES in to see a man standing at the window inside; it is Art; he is scowling grimly.

DISSOLVE:

276   EXT. WINDOW IN SCIENCE BUILDING - NIGHT - CLOSE SHOT

In the dark window Art can still be seen, he looks agitated, angry; he is smoking a cigarette; suddenly he quickly puts it out and leans back into the shadows - watching the garden below...

277   EXT. LAWN - NIGHT - LONG SHOT - ART'S P.O.V.

Bryan and Diane - arm in arm - are walking towards the building.

278   INT. CORRIDOR WINDOW - NIGHT - MED. SHOT

Abruptly Art turns from the window and walks down the corridor.

279   INT. STAIR WELL LANDING - NIGHT

It is dark; Art comes quietly to the landing; he stops and listens; from the stair well voices can be heard.

                    BRYAN (O.S.)
          Good night - Diane...

280   CLOSEUP - ART

He looks jealous and spiteful.

                    DIANE (O.S.)
          Good night - darling!..

Art's face hardens with fury; the sound of a door closing can be heard; then footsteps coming up the stairs; Art silently melts into the dark shadows in a corner; CAMERA FOLLOWS him.

281 WIDER ANGLE

Bryan comes up the stairs; there is a happy little smile on his face. Art is almost invisible in the dark shadows; Bryan pauses on the landing; he looks towards the window...

282 CLOSEUP - ART

He is watching Bryan with hate in his eyes.

283 MED. WIDE SHOT - LANDING

Bryan goes to the window; he opens it; stands for a moment at the low sill looking out into the starry night...

284 MED. CLOSEUP - ART

Standing in the shadows behind Bryan he is watching him tensely; all his hate, jealousy and envy are mirrored on his face; slowly he raises his hands before him in a pushing position; little beads of sweat stand out on his forehead, and his eyes burn with malice...

285 ANGLE - ART'S P.O.V.

Bryan is standing at the open window with his back to Art; he is clearly silhouetted against the night sky.

286 MED. CLOSEUP - ART

He is gathering all his courage to rush at his rival and send him plunging to the ground below; he begins to tremble - then he starts forward - but stops; slowly he clenches his fists and lets them sink to his sides; his face muscles work in frustration - as his courage fails him...

287 WIDER ANGLE

Bryan turns from the window - and walks away down the corridor...

288 CLOSEUP - ART

With hate-filled eyes he listens to Bryan's disappearing footsteps.

114.

289 INT. LANDING - NIGHT - MED. SHOT

Art is standing in the shadows; slowly he starts to walk down the corridor.

290 DOLLY SHOT

CAMERA LEADS Art down the corridor; as he passes an open door, there is a faint groan from inside the room; he stops; then he walks over and looks in.

291 INT. STORE ROOM/SICK ROOM - NIGHT   ART'S P.O.V.

It is the little store room that has been made into Nancy's sick room; the light is on; Fanny sits in a chair a little distance away from the bed; she is fast asleep; Nancy lies on the cot; she is still strapped down - but is obviously uncomfortable; she looks at Art with wide, burning eyes; she moans softly; CAMERA DOLLIES in to a MED. CLOSE SHOT.

292 ANOTHER ANGLE

Art is standing next to the bed; he looks down at Nancy.

     ART
    (in a half-whisper;
    bitterly)
You - with your alien mind...You would have had the courage...the guts to do what I want to do -- but can't!..

He turns away to go; suddenly he hesitates; he gets a crafty look on his face; he turns back to the bed.

(The following conversation is conducted in an urgent whisper, so as not to awaken the soundly sleeping Fanny.)

     ART
  Nancy...?

The girl doesn't answer him; she looks steadfastly at him with her burning eyes.

     ART
  <u>Grag</u>?!

For a moment the girl is silent; then she speaks in a curious, controlled manner.

        (CONTINUED)

292 (CONTINUED)

      GRAG/NANCY
  Yes - Dr. Corliss!

Art involuntarily reacts; then he resolutely goes on, urgently...

      ART
  Listen to me, Grag...You need help.
  And I'm in a position to help you.

      GRAG
  How?

      ART
  If I let you enter my body, you
  would be right in the middle of
  your enemies, for they trust me.

      GRAG
  You're not forsaking your friends
  for nothing. What do you want?

      ART
  Bryan destroyed.

      GRAG
  That goes without saying, since
  he's allied with my mortal enemy.

      ART
  Seems like we got the same mortal
  enemy. I want Diane safe.

      GRAG
  She shall be yours. Anything else?

      ART
  I want to be your number one man
  when you take over.

      GRAG
  I couldn't think of a better choice,
  Dr. Corliss. We're made of the same
  stuff - that leaders are made of.
  You know how to let me enter?

      ART
  Yes, but - I don't want to be like
  - her.
    (he indicates Nancy)
  I want our relationship to be like
  Bryan's and Nordot's...

        (CONTINUED)

292   (CONTINUED - 2)

                    GRAG
          It will be. There will be very
          little reaction, for you will not
          be trying to fight me off like she
          has.

                    ART
          We'll show Professor Kenmore a
          thing or two.

Art's greed, spite and envy shine in his face; slowly he
walks closer to the possessed girl, who watches him with
burning eyes; the room is deathly quiet - with the ex-
ception of Fanny's heavy breathing - as Art and Nancy/Grag
lock glances; then CAMERA DOLLIES in to a CLOSE SHOT, as
Art bends over the girl - and hesitates...

                                        DISSOLVE:

293   INT. B LABORATORY - DAY - CLOSE SHOT - COMPLICATED GLASS
      TUBE AND BOTTLE STILL

A liquid is being distilled; CAMERA PULLS OUT to a MED.
SHOT as the boiling liquid bubbles and steams through
the glass tubing...

Watkins and Bryan are watching the process intently; a
small amount of liquid has already formed in the end
product test tube; Watkins fills the syringe from this
container; Bryan holds one of the rubber covered test
tubes for him, while the Professor injects the liquid
into the test tube. For a brief moment it seethes and
boils in the dark liquid, then it calms down - and the
dark liquid in the test tube becomes clear...

                    WATKINS
                  (impatiently)
          Nothing!

Impulsively he rips the end product test tube from the
still and in a burst of uncontrolled frustration he
shatters it in the sink. Bryan regards him soberly, as
the older man stiff-legged stalks to the window and
stands looking out for a moment.

CAMERA FOLLOWS, as Bryan goes to another table, where a
different chemical apparatus is set up...Here, too, a
liquid id steaming through...

                                        (CONTINUED)

293 (CONTINUED)

>   BRYAN
>   (quietly)
>   I've gone as far as I can with
>   the potentiator, Norot...I don't
>   know where to go from here...
>
>   NOROT
>   Let us test the preparation...
>
>   BRYAN
>   I'll use a fair-sized amount...

Bryan begins to draw off some of the steaming liquid into a large flask.

294 ANOTHER ANGLE

The door in the back opens, and Tim comes in; he is carrying a small, but heavy centrifuge machine; he walks towards Bryan.

>   TIM
>   Where do you want this?
>
>   BRYAN
>   Oh, the centrifuge...Put it down
>   right here...There's a plug under
>   the table top...

Tim makes for the table; suddenly he stops - and lets out a healthy sneeze - unable to cover his mouth, as he has both hands full carrying the centrifuge.

>   BRYAN
>   Gesundtheit!
>
>   TIM
>   Sorry...

He places the centrifuge on the table and plugs it in, while Bryan places several test tubes with various liquids in the machine to be 'whirled', during:

>   BRYAN
>   Caught a cold?
>
>   TIM
>   It's that chilly night air most
>   likely...standing guard on the
>   gate...

(CONTINUED)

294 (CONTINUED)

Watkins joins them; he has calmed down.

> WATKINS
> Keep this batch in the centrifuge a full fifteen minutes...

> BRYAN
> Right...

Watkins picks up a clipboard with some papers on it; he studies them; Bryan starts the centrifuge; the tubes begin to whirl around with ever increasing speed; Tim watches with interest...

> TIM
> Quite a gadget!

Bryan returns to the flask with the steaming potentiator liquid; CAMERA FOLLOWS him; Bryan bends over the flask; the vapors rise and drift to envelop him...Suddenly he straightens up with a jerk...stiffly he turns; his face is distorted with strain; he takes one step...

> "BRYAN"
> Tim!

...and he collapses on the floor!

Immediately Tim and Watkins are at his side; he is unconscious; they sit him up.

> TIM
> (anxiously)
> Bryan!..Bryan!..

Slowly Bryan opens his eyes...

> WATKINS
> Bryan! Are you all right? What happened?

Bryan passes a hand over his eyes; he draws himself up...

> BRYAN
> I don't know...Norot was in control...

> WATKINS
> Norot!

> TIM
> Ask him what happened...

(CONTINUED)

294 (CONTINUED - 2)

>   BRYAN
>   Norot...

They all wait anxiously for Norot to respond; there is only tense silence...

>   BRYAN
>   (anxiously)
>   Norot! Take control!..

Slowly Bryan's eyes close; his head sinks down; he seems to sag; then he painfully raises his head and looks at Watkins.

>   WATKINS
>   Norot?
>
>   NOROT
>   Yes...
>
>   WATKINS
>   What went wrong?
>
>   NOROT
>   I was attacked...almost killed!
>
>   WATKINS
>   Attacked! Killer! By whom?...By
>   what?!
>
>   NOROT
>   (regaining his
>   strength)
>   With every breath thousands of germs
>   and viruses enter Bryan's body...
>   I have been able to destroy them all
>   easily...
>
>   WATKINS
>   (impatiently)
>   Yes, yes...What are you getting
>   at?
>
>   NOROT
>   One is more abundant than any other...
>   It was never a danger to me before...
>   But suddenly its strength surged...
>   and I was nearly destroyed!
>
>   WATKINS
>   (excited)
>   Which one, Norot? Which virus??!

(CONTINUED)

294 (CONTINUED - 3)

>   NOROT
> Just now - it was expelled in
> great quantity - by Tim.

>   TIM
> Me! I just sneezed!

>   WATKINS
> Of course! The cold virus! The
> common cold!

>   NOROT
> If that's what made Tim sneeze -
> that is the virus!

>   WATKINS
> But what happened? Why should the
> cold virus suddenly become strong
> enough to attack you?...

Bryan suddenly sits up excitedly, as Bryan himself takes control.

>   BRYAN
>   (excitedly)
> The _potentiator_!

>   WATKINS
> The potentiator?...

>   BRYAN
> I was inhalting its vapors! The
> potentiator must have acted upon
> the viruses - given them sudden,
> fantastic strength! Norot! Is
> that the answer?...

>   NOROT
> Yes, Bryan...If such viruses -
> given strength with the potentiator
> - invade the bodies of the hosts in
> force - none of my race should be
> able to defeat them...It would be
> for each of them, like a man fighting
> a tiger with his bare hands..._He
> would be destroyed_!

>   WATKINS
> Tim! Don't go away!..

Bryan relaxes, as Norot withdraws control.

(CONTINUED)

294 (CONTINUED - 4)

                    BRYAN
          It'll work!..We can create a
          living-virus concentrate - but
          instead of making the virus more
          gentle - we'll make it stronger...
          A thousandfold more virulent!

                    TIM
          I get it! You'll put that stuff
          into the infected people - and
          it'll kill the alien micro-men!
          Kind of like throwing down a cat
          to rid the basement of rats!

                    BRYAN
          That's it exactly! And the host
          won't be harmed...We can cope with
          a cold!

                    TIM
          Okay! You can have as many of my
          cold germs as you want! When do
          we start?

                    BRYAN
          Right now!..

                                        DISSOLVE:

295 EXT. GATE BARRICADE - DAY - MED. SHOT

     Sammy and Bernie, armed with rifles, are on guard; Sammy
     looks out over the landscape.

                    SAMMY
          Looks peaceful out there...You think
          so?

                    BERNIE
                  (dryly)
          About as peaceful as no-man's-land!
                  (he jerks his thumb)
          That tractor working the field over
          there hasn't budged for hours!

     Sammy gives Bernie a quick look; then they both look out...

296 EXT. FIELDS - DAY - EXTREME LONG SHOT - GATE P.O.V.

     In the distance a tractor can be seen standing in a half-
     worked field.

297   FULL SHOT - TRACTOR

   Two men are sitting or leaning, motionless, on the tractor.

298   CLOSE TWO SHOT

   The two men look grim - and almost 'robot-like'; they do not move, but simply stare towards the gate; CAMERA PANS off them - down to two rifles leaning against the tractor! CAMERA then PANS RIGHT, off the tractor to a LONG SHOT; in the distance can be seen a road; a car is halted there...

                              DISSOLVE:

299   EXT. ROAD - DAY - FULL SHOT - CAR STANDING ON ROAD

   The hood has been put up; a man stands near the exposed engine; he, too, looks grim and motionless, as he watches the distant gate; CAMERA PANS off him to the car window; another man sits inside; through the window sticks the gleaming barrel of a rifle!

   CAMERA PANS RIGHT, off the car to a LONG SHOT of the fields; there are several telephone poles to be seen...

                              DISSOLVE:

300   EXT. TELEPHONE POLES ON FIELD - SUNSET - MED. SHOT

   A jeep is parked beneath the nearest pole; two men are visible; one is up the pole, the other stands at the foot; both are grimly watching the campus...

301   SHOT - MAN ON POLE - GROUND P.O.V.

   He is secured to the pole with his safety belt; in his hands he holds a rifle...CAMERA PANS down to a CLOSE SHOT of the man below; he, too, has a rifle...CAMERA then PANS off the men towards a small stand of trees in the b.g.

                              DISSOLVE:

302   EXT. EDGE OF WOODS - NIGHT - MED. SHOT

   Two hunters sit quietly - ominously - in a small blind; both have shotguns lying across their knees...

                              (CONTINUED)

302   (CONTINUED)

    CAMERA DOLLIES in on one of the guns to a CLOSEUP of the hands holding it firmly...

                                  DISSOLVE:

303   INT. B LABORATORY - NIGHT - CLOSE SHOT - HANDS HOLDING A TEST TUBE

    CAMERA PULLS BACK to reveal Bryan - holding the test tube - Watkins, Art and Tim.

                BRYAN
             (solemnly)
       Here it is!..<u>Our weapon!</u>

              WATKINS
       Diane should have Nancy ready for us...I'll check...You bring the concentrate, Bryan...Come on, Tim...

Watkins and Tim leave; Bryan begins to transfer the liquid from the test tube to a small bottle with a rubber cover; CAMERA DOLLIES in to a TWO SHOT, during:

                ART
       I don't like it...

              BRYAN
             (gravely)
       It has to be done...

                ART
       Using the girl as a guinea pig!.. Can't we test it some other way?

              BRYAN
       How, Art? We have no time to try... Don't you think I've racked my brain to find some other solution? There isn't any!

                ART
             (grimly)
       Then...you're going ahead - with Nancy?

              BRYAN
       It's our only chance...For her - and for all of us!..

                                (CONTINUED)

303 (CONTINUED)

>   ART
>   Playing kind of fast and loose
>   with a human life, aren't you?
>   Quite a responsibility...

>   BRYAN
>   (he looks haunted)
>   I _have_ a conscience, Art!

>   ART
>   What if you kill her?!

Bryan holds up the little bottle: it is full now...

>   BRYAN
>   It's a responsibility I'll have
>   to shoulder...

Art glares at him, then he turns abruptly and stalks out.

304   INT. STORE/SICK ROOM - NIGHT - MED. SHOT

Diane and Fanny are hovering over the cot on which Nancy lies - still restrained by the bonds; the girl looks completely expressionless; one of her arms is bared... Watkins and Tim stand by; Bryan enters with the bottle.

>   BRYAN
>   Is she ready?

>   DIANE
>   Yes.

Watkins takes the bottle from Bryan; he goes to the little medicine table and fills a syringe with the liquid, during:

Bryan goes to stand at the foot of the cot; he looks with compassion at Nancy; suddenly he stiffens and grows somber - as Norot takes over control.

>   NOROT
>   Grag!

The girl instantly fixes Bryan/Norot with a penetrating stare; briefly she strains against her bonds; then as quickly she subsides; she speaks with a cold, snarling voice.

>   NANCY/GRAG
>   You have taken yourself a fine
>   host, Norot!

(CONTINUED)

304 (CONTINUED)

>   NOROT
>   A host with whom I work in perfect
>   cooperation - to destroy you - and
>   your kind, Grag!
>
>   NANCY/GRAG
>   Traitor!
>
>   NOROT
>   To the principle of enslavement...
>   Yes!

The girl sneers contemptuously; Watkins moves up with the syringe; he tests it; then he nods to Tim.

>   WATKINS
>   Hold her arm still, will you...
>   But be careful!

Tim moves to obey.

>   NOROT
>   You are about to die, Grag!

Again the girl makes a sudden, brief effort to break from her bonds...

>   NANCY/GRAG
>   Even if you do destroy me - you
>   can't kill us all!

305 ANOTHER ANGLE

Watkins bends over the girl's exposed arm; he inserts the needle - and injects the concentrate; Diane moves closer to Bryan, who relaxes, as Norot relinquishes control...

Watkins removes the syringe...

306 CLOSEUP - NANCY

The girl's eyes are opened wide; little beads of sweat stand out on her forehead; she is breathing heavily through her half-open mouth...Suddenly an agonized growl starts deep in her throat; her eyes open even wider in abyssmal terror, as the tortured growl turns into a hideous scream - torn from her snarling lips!..

307 WIDER ANGLE

Diane impulsively moves to help the girl, but Bryan restrains her.

          BRYAN
    No, Diane!

Diane looks up at him in angusih.

          BRYAN
    We can do nothing!

          DIANE
    But - she may die!

          BRYAN
    Her body is a battlefield...We
    can only hope the right forces
    win...But we can do nothing to
    help!

They all watch Nancy with haunted expressions; Diane turns away to bury her face on Bryan's shoulder; Fanny crosses herself; Tim looks shaken and pale...CAMERA DOLLIES in to a CLOSEUP of Nancy; she is moaning and writhing violently in her bonds; she gnashes her teeth - and foam begins to form at the corners of her mouth...

          DISSOLVE:

308 INT. SHERIFF'S OFFICE - NIGHT - CLOSEUP - SERGEANT STRAUSS

His face looks icy, hard and cruel.

          MORGAN (O.S.)
    In about four days -- the community
    will be ours - completely!..

309 CLOSEUP - OFFICER LAWSON - OVERLAPPING

He, too, looks ruthless and malevolent.

          MORGAN (O.S.)
    Whatever we do - whatever happens
    here...will not be known elsewhere...

310 CLOSEUP - MAN - OVERLAPPING

It is the man who had his shirt ripped by Strauss; he, too, has a brutal, harsh expression on his face.

          (CONTINUED)

127.

310   (CONTINUED)

                    MORGAN (O.S.)
            ...our presence will not be be-
            trayed to the rest of this world...
            until we're ready for it...

311   MED. GROUP SHOT - OVERLAPPING

      Morgan is talking to a group of men and women; they all
      look grim and menacing

                    MORGAN
            Four days from now...Saturday -
            at midnight -

312   CLOSEUP - MORGAN - OVERLAPPING

      He looks utterly ruthless - almost inhuman...

                    MORGAN
            We attack!

313   SHOCK CUT

      INT. STORE/SICK ROOM - NIGHT - CLOSE SHOT - MEDICINE
      TABLE

      With an ear-shattering crash, part of the wooden cot
      comes smashing down on the table, rushing the bottles
      on it...

314   WIDER ANGLE

      The room is a shambles; the cot on which Nancy was lying
      is demolished - the bedding torn to rags; in a far cor-
      ner Diane and Fanny cower in terror; panting - wild-
      eyed - her night clothes ripped - her hair in wild dis-
      array - Nancy stands at the table, facing them...Free!
      She sways a little; then she slowly, inexorably moves
      towards the two petrified women...her hands - bent into
      claws - are slowly raised before her...

315   ANOTHER ANGLE

      Suddenly the door bursts open; Bryan, Watkins and Art
      rush into the room; Nancy whirls upon the intruders...

      Bryan - holding back Watkins and Art - takes a step
      towards her; he speaks sharply - with the voice of
      Norot...
                                              (CONTINUED)

315 (CONTINUED)

>   NOROT
>   Grag!

The girl bares her teeth in a vicious snarl; again she staggers - then she slowly moves towards the three men...

But suddenly she looks stricken; she gasps - and keels over in a dead faint...

Watkins starts for her, but Bryan/Norot stops him; slowly the young man kneels by the girl; he takes her head gently; the girl's eyelids flutter - and slowly open...For a moment she looks up at Bryan/Norot - then at the others - and quietly she begins to weep...

>   NOROT
>   Grag - is dead!
>
>   WATKINS
>   It worked! We can kill the alien
>   micro-men...

316 CLOSE SHOT - ART

He reacts sharply to Watkins' excited outburst.

317 WIDER ANGLE

Diane walks over to Bryan and Nancy; Bryan relaxes, as Norot retreats from his mind.

>   DIANE
>   Let me...She needs rest...
>
>   BRYAN
>   What happened?
>
>   DIANE
>   She seemed almost in a coma - after
>   being delirious...Then suddenly she
>   tore at the bonds so violently -
>   that she broke the cot itself - and
>   got free...It happened so fast...
>
>   WATKINS
>   Grag's last, dying effort...

(CONTINUED)

317　(CONTINUED)

                BRYAN
Put her to bed, Diane...Fanny'll help...
        (he stands up)
Now that we <u>have</u> our weapon - we'll have to decide how to <u>use</u> it!..

                      DISSOLVE:

318　INT. WATKINS' OFFICE - MED. SHOT

The drapes are drawn at the window; the lights are on; Watkins, Bryan, Tim and Art are present; they all look dead tired; Watkins is sitting at his desk; it is covered with papers and notes...

              WATKINS
...That leaves only one problem to be solved...

                ART
The most important one!

              WATKINS
...<u>How</u> to administer the preparation - to every single person in the community!

                ART
We obviously can't do it by injection!

There is a knock on the door.

              WATKINS
Yes, yes...Come in!

The door opens and Diane enters with a tray with steaming coffee and toast.

               DIANE
Are you still at it?...

She puts down the tray and walks to the window.

               DIANE
Do you realize you've been working all night?

                      (CONTINUED)

318 (CONTINUED)

She draws the drapes aside; the sunlight streams into the room.

                BRYAN
We haven't quite finished yet...

                DIANE
Well, you'd better take a coffee break...Everybody has to eat and drink - even scientists!

Bryan starts; he whirls on Diane.

                BRYAN
What did you say!???

                DIANE
              (firmly)
I said: Drink your coffee!

                BRYAN
              (with mounting
              excitement)
And you are so right! Everybody should drink their coffee! Or tea! Or just plain water!!

Impulsively he gives the girl an enthusiastic hug; Diane gently disengages herself, laughing.

                DIANE
              (mischievously)
Bryan! What will Norot say!

                WATKINS
What is your idea, Bryan?

                BRYAN
We don't have to inject anybody! Our preparation can be administered to them in another way...In the water they drink!

                TIM
In the water?...

                BRYAN
All we have to do is dump a concentrate in the water supply!..It'll multiply and spread by itself!.. within a couple of days our virus will be fighting in the body of every man, woman and child in the community!

                (CONTINUED)

318   (CONTINUED)

>   DIANE
>   (to Bryan)
> What about you - and Norot?

>   BRYAN
> From now on, my only liquid re-
> freshment will be...<u>distilled
> water.</u>

                              DISSOLVE:

319   INT. B LABORATORY - DAY - CLOSE SHOT - CHEMICAL APPARATUS

It is going full blast; liquids boil and seethe in the maze of glass tubing and flasks...CAMERA PULLS BACK to a MED. SHOT.

Watkins, Bryan and Art are busy at the apparatus, which is part of their set-up for the manufacturing of their concentration...On one of the tables stand row upon row of bottles filled with a lightly colored liquid. Art is standing at this table, keeping track of the amount of concentrate made.

>   ART
> Has anyone figured out yet, what
> to carry all this stuff in, to get
> it to the reservoir?

>   BRYAN
> Everyone's looking for something
> to use as a container...

>   WATKINS
> It will probably have to be a choice
> between Sammy's old milk can - or
> Bernie's fire extinguisher...or both.

He nods towards another table where these two objects can be seen.

>   BRYAN
> I don't like either...Too unwieldy...
> too heavy...too noisy...We may not
> have far to go - but we'll have to
> do a real job of silent infiltra-
> tion...

320   ANOTHER ANGLE

The door to the lab opens and Tim comes in; he is carrying two car tire inner tubes; he walks to the table - and throws the tubes in front of the men.

>   TIM
>   (cheerfully)
> Well - Here are your containers!

>   WATKINS
> Inner tubes!?

>   TIM
> Sure! They're strong - easy to carry - silent when you drag them along the ground...and the two of them will hold more stuff than you calculated you'd need!

>   BRYAN
> Tim - you're a genius!

Tim beams.

>   TIM
> Naw!...Just been around machinery and trucks a long time...I figured we could carry one apiece...

>   BRYAN
> Right...

>   TIM
> All we have to do is slash them open with a knife before throwing them in...

>   ART
>   (determinatedly)
> Bryan - I want to go with you and Tim...

>   BRYAN
> It won't be necessary, Art...Besides, you'll be needed here - in case of attack!

>   ART
>   (persuasively)
> If there *is* an all out attack, one man more *or* less won't matter...The important thing is to get those things...
>   (he indicates the tubes)
> ...to the water...

(CONTINUED)

320 (CONTINUED)

> WATKINS
> Art is right, Bryan...We'll manage here...

> BRYAN
> Okay, Art...We'll be ready tonight...

321 EXT. GIMMICK ON WALL TOP - NIGHT - CLOSE SHOT

CAMERA PANS down to the little door in the wall that Bryan and Tim used before. Bryan and Tim stand smoking at the door; both of them are clad in dark, tight fitting clothes; their faces are smeared with black, commando fashion; they wear heavy socks over their shoes; both Bryan and Tim wear a knife in their belts; on the ground before them lie the two inner tubes; they both look fat and heavy...

Watkins comes up to the two men; they all talk in half whispers...

> BRYAN
> Where's Art?

> WATKINS
> He'll be right here...He went to get his knife...

> BRYAN
> He'd better hurry...We want to take advantage of the dark...

322 INT. WATKINS' OFFICE - NIGHT - MED. CLOSE SHOT - DIANE

She is at the desk; the room is lit by one lamp only; Diane is gathering together the papers on Watkins' desk; she picks them up and starts for the open door to the dark corridor outside the room...As she reaches the door the figure of a man suddenly steps into it - blocking her way; (shoot for shock value); the man is clad in a black shirt; dark pants; and his face is smeared with black; it is Art; in his belt he has a knife; Diane gives a small cry as she stumbles back; she drops the papers - then recognizes Art...

> DIANE
> Art! You startled me!

(CONTINUED)

322 (CONTINUED)

Art looks ominous; he doesn't make a sound; slowly he advances upon Diane.

          DIANE
      (growing frightened)
  What's the matter?...Art?!..

The man advances steadily upon her...

          ART
  I told you to stay away from Bryan!
  And you needn't deny it. I made it
  a point to watch you!..

          DIANE
  No, Art!..**No**!..

Suddenly Art grabs for the girl; she twists away, but he catches hold of her arm - and pulls her roughly to him; Diane struggles like a fury; her hand grabs hold of Art's shirt front - and as she fights, the shirt is ripped open! Diane gasps.

There on Art's chest is the tell-tale rash!

          DIANE
      (in a terrified
      whisper)
  Grag!

Art keeps a firm grip on the girl.

          ART
      (hoarsely; excited)
  Yes, Diane! Grag **is** with me! I
  let him join me! **I wanted him**!

          DIANE
      (horrified)
  Oh, God!...

          ART
  Listen, Diane...Forget about Bryan
  ...Forget about the others...With
  Grag as our ally, you and I can
  have everything in the world we want!

          DIANE
      (struggling)
  Let me go!..

                  (CONTINUED)

322 (CONTINUED - 2)

      ART
  Everything. The whole world!

      DIANE
No!

      ART
  You'll change your mind! There is
  nothing I won't be able to do!

      DIANE
    (becomes hysterical
    with fear and panic)
No! No! No!

Suddenly she wrenches herself free; she starts at once to let out a scream, but Art - anticipating her - jabs a vicious rabbit punch to her neck...Without a sound the girl sinks to the floor...Art starts to bend over her; there is the sound of a door being slammed o.s.; Art looks up quickly - and hurries out...

323 EXT. DOOR IN WALL - NIGHT MED. SHOT

Bryan, Tim and Watkins are waiting; Art comes hurrying up; he is wearing a heavy sweater.

      TIM
  What kept you?

      ART
  Had to find my knife...How about
  a gun?

      BRYAN
  We aren't taking any.

      ART
  No guns?

      BRYAN
  We'll have to reach the dam without
  being seen...We can't <u>shoot</u> our way
  through...The moment we fire a shot
  out there - we're lost!

      ART
  We should have guns...

        (CONTINUED)

323 (CONTINUED)

>   BRYAN
> We've only got four...They stay
> here. To protect the girls.

Art scowls, but says no more.

Bryan is looking expectantly towards the building.

>   BRYAN
> Did you see Diane?

>   ART
> She's looking after Nancy...

Bryan looks disappointed.

>   BRYAN
> Okay...Let's go!

He and Tim each take one of the full inner tubes and drape them around their necks; then Bryan opens the door cautiously and looks out; he turns to the others.

>   BRYAN
> All clear...

>   WATKINS
> Good luck - to all of you!

Cautiously the three men slip out through the little door; Watkins bolts it behind them...

324 EXT. SHRUBBERY OUTSIDE THE WALL - NIGHT - MED. WIDE SHOT

Bryan, Tim and Art run in a crouch from the little door in the wall; Bryan and Tim carry the tubes; Art brings up the rear; they reach a small depression in the underbrush and fall to the ground; after a moment they cautiously begin to crawl towards an open clearing ahead...

325 CLOSE SHOT - BRYAN

Silently he crawls along the ground; he stops - immobile - to listen.

326 INT. WATKINS' OFFICE - NIGHT - CLOSE SHOT - DIANE

She is lying, unconscious, on the floor just inside the door in the dimly lit room; all at once the light is turned on....

328   TWO SHOT

With a small moan Diane begins to come to; she is groggy...

                WATKINS
      What happened? What's wrong?
      Diane!..

Suddenly everything comes back to the girl; with horror mirrored in her eyes, she grabs on to Watkins.

                DIANE
         (frantically)
      Stop them! Don't let them go!

                WATKINS
      Stop who?

                DIANE
      Bryan! Dad!..and - Art!..

                WATKINS
      But - they've already gone!

Diane buries her face in her hands.

                DIANE
      Oh, God!...

                WATKINS
         (alarmed)
      What is it, Diane?

Diane looks up at Watkins - her face is chalk white, her eyes haunted.

                DIANE
      He is - one of them!..

                WATKINS
         (urgently)
      Who? What is it???

                DIANE
      Art! He let himself be infected
      - by Grag!

Watkins looks stunned.

                WATKINS
         (dazed)
      Your...brother...

                            (CONTINUED)

328   (CONTINUED)

                    DIANE
          They're carrying - perhaps the only
          hope unsuspecting mankind has...
          And - the enemy walks with them!..
                (she turns to Watkins)
          We must warn them!...

                    WATKINS
                (resolutely)
          They haven't been gone long...Per-
          haps I can catch up with them.

                    DIANE
          You?!..

     Watkins starts to shrug out of his white laboratory
     smock...

                    WATKINS
                (with a glint in
                 his eye)
          Help me get ready. We have no time
          to lose!

329 EXT. SHRUB COVERED HILLSIDE - NIGHT - CLOSE SHOT - BUSH

     Cautiously it is parted; Bryan's black smeared face peers
     through.

330 ANOTHER ANGLE - WIDER SHOT

     Bryan lies behind the small bush; further back lie Tim
     and Art; Bryan waves them on; they all begin to crawl
     ahead. (The sound of rushing water is heard throughout
     the following scenes.)

331 CLOSE SHOT - ART

     He looks worried and nervous; he keeps looking around -
     and back.

332 WIDE ANGLE - (LOCATION: MINT CANYON AQUADUCT CASCADE,
     L.A.)

     The three men can be seen crawling up the hillside; not
     far from them an aquaduct cascade rushes down the steep
     slope to disappear under a bridge over the highway below.

                                             (CONTINUED)

332   (CONTINUED)

(The cascade is used to aerate the water; it is a steep, broad concrete spillway; in the cement bottom are set thousands of sharp and jagged rocks; the water cascades from the reservoir above in a shallow stream over these rocks, being churned to white foam by the craggy points; it is a spectacular display of wild power - and lethal, potential danger!)

333   THREE SHOT

Tim and Bryan are in the f.g.; Art is in the b.g.; he keeps looking towards the road below.

                    TIM
            The dam is just above...

                    BRYAN
            We must get the stuff into the
            reservoir itself...We'll follow
            the cascade up...

                    TIM
            Let's go.

                    BRYAN
            Careful. That highway down there
            is the main road to the campus...
            They're sure to patrol it!

                    TIM
            Okay...

They start up the hill; Art reluctantly follows.

334   ANOTHER ANGLE - WIDE SHOT DOWN THE HILLSIDE TO ROAD BELOW

In the f.g. Bryan and Tim make their way up the hillside next to the roaring cascade; Art is quite a bit further back...

Suddenly on the road below - a car slowly rounds the bend and comes into view; it is a police patrol car; the men inside are playing a searchlight on the road shoulders as the car slowly drives on; the three men on the hillside flatten themselves on the ground... All at once Art jumps to his feet and bellows at the top of his lungs.

                    ART
            Here!..Up here!..On the hill!..

335 CLOSEUP - BRYAN

He looks shocked; incredulous.

>   BRYAN
>   Art!

336 SHOT ACROSS ART TO CAR ON ROAD

The patrol car stops; the searchlight finds Art; all at once he is silhouetted against the bright light...

>   ART
>   Up there!
>   (he waves towards
>   Bryan and Tim)
>   Two of them!! Stop them! Stop...

Suddenly a few shots ring out from the car; Art at once hits the dirt; from the car three men come racing up the hillside - shooting...

337 TWO SHOT - BRYAN AND TIM

They are crouched, concealed behind some shrubbery; the whine of bullets passing over their heads can be heard.

>   BRYAN
>   They got - Art!

Tim is shrugging off his tube with the vaccine concentration; he pushes it over towards Bryan.

>   TIM
>   Here...Take this...First chance
>   you get - take off for the dam!

338 WIDER ANGLE

The three men from the patrol car are nearly at Bryan's and Tim's hiding place; we recognize Morgan, Lawson and another man from town...As they are almost upon the two hidden men, Tim suddenly jumps up with a maddened roar; the men are taken by surprise; Tim delivers a mighty blow to the one man's head, sending him crashing to the ground; then - before either Morgan or Lawson can bring their guns to bear - he grapples with them both.

>   TIM
>   (roaring)
>   Get going, Bryan!

(CONTINUED)

338   (CONTINUED)

Bryan jumps up, carrying both the heavy tubes; for a moment he hesitates - then he starts to scramble up the hillside towards the dam and reservoir above...

Further down Art gets to his feet - and unhampered by any extra weight he rushes in pursuit of Bryan - while Tim battles furiously with Morgan and Lawson...

339   THE FIGHT

The fight will be routined...Tim fights like a madman; all his pent up feelings of guilt and responsibility are being taken out on the two men; he manages to land a hard blow to the solar plexus of Lawson; the man doubles up in pain; but the effort sends Tim's knife flying from his belt; Morgan's and Lawson's guns have long since been lost in the weeds - but Morgan now quickly grabs the knife; Tim has his back to the roaring cascade; Morgan rushes at him with the knife murderously held out before him; in the last possible moment Tim twists aside and bends over; Morgan misses his target - and pitches headlong into the cascade!..

At once he is swept along by the tremendous force of the water down the spillway - literally being ripped to shreds on the thousands of razor-sharp rock points!.. His screams of anguish are quickly drowned out by the roar of the swirling water...

340   THE HILLSIDE

Bryan is climbing - higher and higher; but Art has closed the gap between them.

341   THE FIGHT

Lawson has recovered enough to attack Tim again; they are fighting violently; on the ground the first man, Tim knocked out, begins to stir; groggily he sits up; on the ground next to him lies Tim's lost knife; he reaches out and takes it...

Tim has Lawson in a bear-like locking hold; with all his might he strains to break the man; behind his massive back the other enemy gets to his feet; he raises the knife to plunge it into Tim's back - when out of nowhere a heavy stick crashes down upon his head (shoot for shock value), and he collapses instantly; at the same moment Tim lets go the weakened Lawson long enough to deliver a mighty blow to his jaw, which sends the man sprawling, unconscious...

(CONTINUED)

341   (CONTINUED)

Tim turns - and discovers the man who saved his life; it is Watkins; he looks flushed - almost excited; he holds a thick stick in his hands; Tim at once takes in the situation, realizing that the Professor saved his life, when he sees the unconscious man on the ground, still clutching the knife...

The two men look at each other with new respect.

>TIM
> Professor!..

>WATKINS
>(urgently)
>Where are the others?

>TIM
>Up there!

He points.

342   LONG SHOT - HILLCREST - TIM'S P.O.V.

Bryan - still carrying the two tubes - can be seen disappearing over the crest - closely followed by Art.

343   MED. SHOT - TIM AND WATKINS

>WATKINS
>Let's go!

They start up the hill...

344   EXT. THE DAM - NIGHT - LONG SHOT

It is not a large dam with a small reservoir behind it; a guard rail runs along the top; Bryan comes running out on the dam with the two tubes; Art is right behind him; he reaches him - and jumps him...

345   CLOSER ANGLE - THE FIGHT

The fight will be routined...Art fights with a viciousness and brutality which is almost inhuman; Bryan drops one of the tubes and manages to get out of the other hanging around his neck; Art has pulled his knife; with a snarl he attacks Bryan; Bryan desperately twists

(CONTINUED)

345   (CONTINUED)

aside; instead of hitting Bryan; Art's knife rips open the inner tube Bryan is holding; losing his balance because of the unexpected, slight resistance, Art grabs for the slashed tube spilling concentrate; with a cry of anguish he trips and falls backwards over the guardrail, tumbling into the dark water below - carrying with him the tube pouring the concentration into the reservoir!..Hesitating only long enough to slash the other tube with his own knife and hurling it into the water, Bryan jumps up on the railing - and dives into the reservoir!..

346   EXT. RESERVOIR BANK - NIGHT - MED. SHOT

Small trees come almost right down to the bank; Bryan is in the water at the bank trying to lift Art up on dry land; Art is unconscious; there is a small movement in the brush; Bryan stiffens - but it is Tim and Watkins; they help Bryan bring Art up; in the distance can be heard the roar of motors and the sounds of faint cries...

                    TIM
                (worriedly)
            Is he okay?

                    BRYAN
            Don't know...He swallowed a lot of
            water - and concentrate!

                    WATKINS
            What about you?

                    BRYAN
            I kept my mouth closed...don't think
            I got any...

Bryan turns to Tim.

                    BRYAN (cont'd)
            Give me a hand, Tim...

Bryan and Tim prop the unconscious Art up between them.

347   ANOTHER ANGLE

In the f.g. Bryan and Tim, holding Art, start away from the reservoir bank, following Watkins into the forest growth. Art is beginning to regain consciousness; he is coughing weakly; in the b.g. the dam can be seen;

                                            (CONTINUED)

347   (CONTINUED)

a few small figures, silhouetted against the sky, can be made out running out upon the dam; as Art again coughs, they stop; suddenly there are a couple of sharp reports; from the muzzles of the rifles held by the little figures on the dam bright fire balls belch...At the same instant the dazed Art jerks in spasms as a bullet or two slam into his back!

                    BRYAN
          Get down!

At once the men hit the ground. Bryan and Tim anxiously examine Art.

348   CLOSER SHOT

Bryan quickly examines the wounds in Art's back; he stiffens and looks up at Tim.

                    TIM
          Is he...?

Bryan gravely nods his head...A few more shots ring out and the bullets whine through the air over the men's heads.

                    TIM
          Let's get out of here!

They quickly start into the thicket...

                                        DISSOLVE:

349   INT. WATKINS' OFFICE - NIGHT - CLOSE SHOT - DIANE - PULL BACK

Present are Diane, Watkins, Bryan and Tim. The men are still clad in their 'infiltration outfits'; they look bedraggled and worn.

                    DIANE
              (she looks haunted)
          ...he did it of his own free will!
          He deliberately allied himself
          with - Grag!

                    BRYAN
          And his own allies took his life...

                                        (CONTINUED)

349   (CONTINUED)

                    TIM
          What I don't understand is...If Art
          was controlled by Grag - why didn't
          he kill us all before?

                    BRYAN
          He never had a chance...He had to
          be absolutely sure of getting all
          of us - before exposing himself -
          or we would have destroyed him...
          His best bet was to do just what
          he did; lie low until he could get
          help...

                    WATKINS
          And all we can do now is hope...and
          wait!

                                        DISSOLVE:

350   EXT. GATEWAY - NIGHT - MED. LONG SHOT

        Bernie and Sammy can be seen guarding the gate.

                                        DISSOLVE:

351   EXT. - SUNRISE OVER THE CAMPUS

                                        DISSOLVE:

352   EXT. GATEWAY - DAY - MED. SHOT

        Bernie and Tim stand - rifles in hand - looking out
        over the empty countryside in front of the gate.

353   EXT. COUNTRYSIDE IN FRONT OF GATE - DAY - PAN SHOT

        It looks peaceful; not a soul is to be seen.

                                        DISSOLVE:

354   EXT. GIMMICK ON TOP OF WALL NEAR GATEWAY - NIGHT -
        CLOSE SHOT

        CAMERA PANS down to a MED. SHOT; Bryan and Bernie are
        on guard.

355   ANOTHER ANGLE - WIDER SHOT

Diane comes walking up to the barricade.

356   TWO SHOT - BRYAN AND DIANE

DIANE
I just thought I'd keep you company for a while...Such a lonely way to spend a Saturday night...out here...

BRYAN
Almost Sunday - isn't it?

DIANE
A few minutes before midnight...
(she looks up at him)
The witching hour!

Bryan looks back at her for a moment - deep into her eyes; then - together - they walk to the barricade.

357   ANOTHER ANGLE - TWO SHOT

DIANE
Bryan - what about - Norot?

BRYAN
He is still with me...Although I am aware of him more and more rarely...
(he gives her a searching look)
Do you mind?

DIANE
(with a little smile)
No, darling. I think of him - almost as part of you...

BRYAN
In a way he is...I have grown and matured in many ways - because of him...My work will take on a new dimension...

(CONTINUED)

357   (CONTINUED)

> DIANE
> Wouldn't it be wonderful, if everyone could have those advantages...Maybe that's what the world needs - a Norot to help us grow up!

> BRYAN
> No, Diane...The human race will remain itself - free and independent...We'll reach our destination in our own way...

Diane shivers slightly; she moves closer to Bryan.

> BRYAN
> Don't you think you'd better go in?

> DIANE
> It's such a lovely night...Let me stay with you!..

358   MED. SHOT

Together Bryan and Diane stand at the barricade.

                                    DISSOLVE:

359   ANOTHER ANGLE - GATEWAY - MORNING - MED. SHOT

Bernie, Bryan and Diane are at the barricade...

Suddenly - from the distance - can be heard the faint sounds of approaching sirens; Bryan starts...

360   CLOSER ANGLE

> BRYAN
> Sirens!..Here they come! Give the signal!

Bernie fires two shots into the air.

> BRYAN
> Diane! Go back in the building!
> Bernie! Take the other side!

                                    (CONTINUED)

360   (CONTINUED)

Bryan runs to one side of the gate; Bernie to the other; the sound of sirens gets louder; Diane stays, in cover behind the wall.

361   EXT. FRONT ENTRANCE TO SCIENCE BUILDING - DAY - MED. SHOT

Tim and Watkins come running out - followed by Nancy and Fanny.

362   EXT. CORNER OF BUILDING - DAY - MED. LONG SHOT

Sammy comes racing around the corner; he carries a hoe.

363   EXT. - DAY - MED. CLOSE SHOT - BRYAN AT THE GATEWAY

He looks out.

364   EXT. ROAD IN FRONT OF GATEWAY - DAY - BRYAN'S P.O.V.

In the distance two vehicles can be seen careening towards the gate.

365   EXT. GATEWAY BARRICADE - DAY - WIDE SHOT

All the men have taken up positions around the barricade; the three women are behind the wall; the sirens sound loud...

              BRYAN
       Hold your fire!

He looks out again.

366   EXT. ROAD IN FRONT OF GATE - DAY

The two vehicles come roaring up - and stop; they are two ambulances; an Attendant jumps from the lead ambulance; he looks at the barricade with puzzled consternation.

            BRYAN (O.S.)
     Hold it! Right there!

367   ANOTHER ANGLE

Carefully Bryan steps from behind the barricade; he carries his rifle - pointed right at the ambulance attendant; the man looks suddenly very nervous.

> BRYAN
> What do you want?

> ATTENDANT
> Watch it, Mister, will you? That thing might go off!..

> BRYAN
> Just stay right there.

> ATTENDANT
> What's going on? What's the matter with you?

> BRYAN
> Where are you from?

> ATTENDANT
> Marysville. Marysville General Hospital. Forty miles south...

> BRYAN
> Why come here?

> ATTENDANT
> We couldn't get you on the phone - we thought you might need help out here...

> BRYAN
> Why?

> ATTENDANT
> Haven't you heard? There's an epidemic going on in Heatherton... The whole community is down with a raging fever...

Bryan suddenly turns to the gateway - at the top of his lungs he shouts...

> BRYAN
> It worked! It worked! Everybody's sick!!

There is an immediate, jubilant response from the barricade...Everyone comes streaming out; the ambulance attendant and the crews are completely taken

(CONTINUED)

367 (CONTINUED)

aback at the display of unrestrained joy over the
news; Bernie is doing a little jig with Sammy;
Fanny embraces the ambulance attendant; everyone
gives vent to the relief and joy they feel...Diane
rushes up to Bryan.

368 TWO SHOT

Diane throws herself into Bryan's arms.

    DIANE
 Oh, darling...Everything'll
 be all right now...
   (she gets a mis-
   chievous gleam in
   her eyes)
 Now - we will have time to tease
 and quarrel!!...

    BRYAN
   (he grins)
 Just so we don't spend _fifty years_
 at it!

And he takes her in his arms...

         FADE OUT:

T H E   E N D

Bear Manor Media

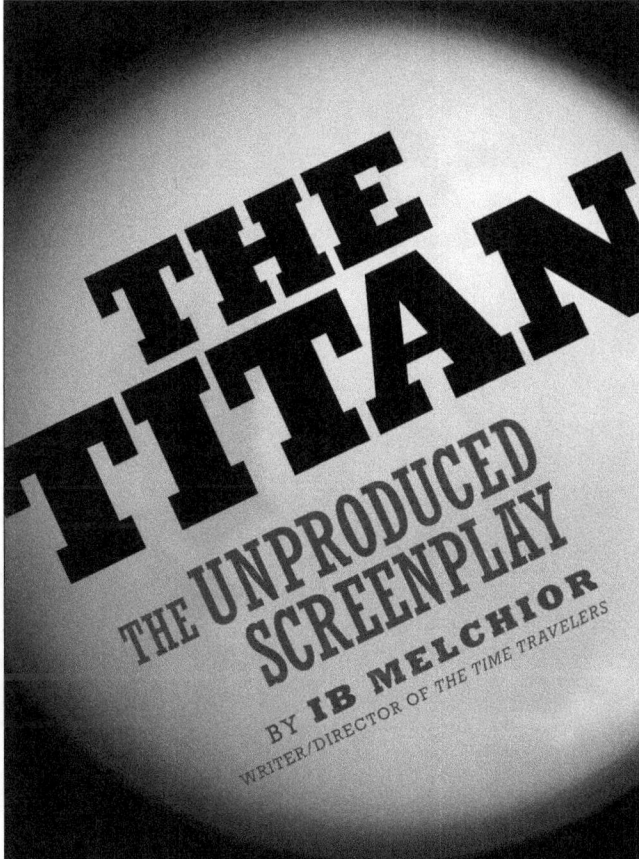
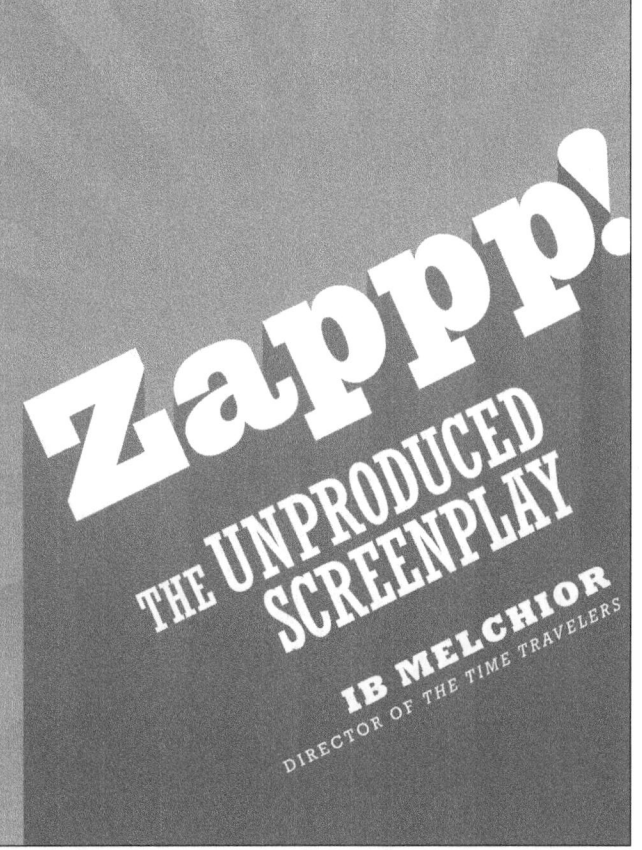

Classic Cinema.
Timeless TV.
Retro Radio.

WWW.BEARMANORMEDIA.COM

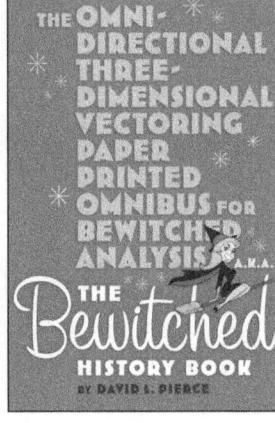

www.ingramcontent.com/pod-product-compliance
Lightning Source LLC
Chambersburg PA
CBHW080436230426
43662CB00015B/2292